Napoleon's Cavalry, Artillery and Technical Corps 1799–1815

Napoleon's Cavalry, Artillery and Technical Corps 1799–1815

History, Organization and Equipment

Gabriele Esposito

Pen & Sword
MILITARY

First published in Great Britain in 2023
by Pen & Sword Military
An imprint of Pen & Sword Books Limited
47 Church Street
Barnsley
South Yorkshire
S70 2AS

Copyright © Gabriele Esposito 2023

ISBN 978 1 39908 980 7

The right of Gabriele Esposito to be identified as
Author of this Work has been asserted by him in accordance
with the Copyright, Designs and Patents Act 1988.

A CIP catalogue record for this book is
available from the British Library

All rights reserved. No part of this book may be reproduced or
transmitted in any form or by any means, electronic or mechanical
including photocopying, recording or by any information storage and
retrieval system, without permission from the Publisher in writing.

Typeset by Mac Style
Printed and bound in India by Replika Press Pvt. Ltd.

Pen & Sword Books Limited incorporates the imprints of Atlas,
Archaeology, Aviation, Discovery, Family History, Fiction, History, Maritime,
Military, Military Classics, Politics, Select, Transport, True Crime, Air World,
Frontline Publishing, Leo Cooper, Remember When, Seaforth Publishing,
The Praetorian Press, Wharncliffe Local History, Wharncliffe Transport,
Wharncliffe True Crime and White Owl.

For a complete list of Pen & Sword titles please contact
PEN & SWORD BOOKS LIMITED
47 Church Street, Barnsley, South Yorkshire, S70 2AS, England
E-mail: enquiries@pen-and-sword.co.uk
Website: www.pen-and-sword.co.uk

Contents

Acknowledgements vii
Introduction viii

Chapter 1   The Cuirassiers   1

Chapter 2   The Carabiniers   14

Chapter 3   The Dragoons   28

Chapter 4   The Lancers   43

Chapter 5   The Hussars   55

Chapter 6   The Mounted Chasseurs   73

Chapter 7   The Artillery   88

Chapter 8   The Technical Corps   111

Chapter 9   The Security Corps   121

Chapter 10   Naval Units   128

Chapter 11   Colonial Units   133

Chapter 12   Foreign Units   141

Bibliography 153
Index 155

Gabriele Esposito is a military historian who works as a freelance author and researcher for some of the most important publishing houses in the military history sector. In particular, he is an expert specializing in uniformology: his interests and expertise range from the ancient civilizations to modern post-colonial conflicts. During recent years he has conducted and published several researches on the military history of the Latin American countries, with special attention on the War of the Triple Alliance and the War of the Pacific. He is among the leading experts on the military history of the Italian Wars of Unification and the Spanish Carlist Wars. His books and essays are published on a regular basis by Pen & Sword Books, Osprey Publishing, Winged Hussar Publishing and Libreria Editrice Goriziana, and he is also the author of numerous military history articles appearing in specialized magazines such as *Ancient Warfare Magazine*, *Medieval Warfare Magazine*, *The Armourer*, *History of War*, *Guerres et Histoire*, *Focus Storia* and *Focus Storia Wars*.

Acknowledgements

This book is dedicated to my parents, Maria Rosaria and Benedetto, for the immense love and great support that they have given me throughout my life. A very special thanks goes to Philip Sidnell, the commissioning editor of my books for Pen & Sword: his love for military history and his passion for publishing are fundamental for the success of our publications. A special mention goes to the production manager of this title, Matt Jones, for his hard work and great competence. Many thanks also to copy-editor Tony Walton, for his expertise, precious help and his friendship. All the pictures published in this book are in the public domain, obtained from the magnificent Digital Collections of the New York Public Library. Anyone with an interest in military history can easily browse the vast contents of the latter at https://digitalcollections.nypl.org/.

Introduction

Napoleon's Grande Armée was one of the most perfect military machines that the history of the world has ever seen, consisting of many different units, each of which was to perform a specific task on the battlefield. The foot regiments of the line and light infantry represented, without doubt, the most important component of the French Army during the Napoleonic period; they were much more numerous than the units of the other branches of service and comprised the bulk of the 'ordinary' soldiers. The other corps of the Grande Armée, such as the cavalry or the artillery, were fundamental not from a quantitative point of view but from a qualitative one: their members were professionals who underwent specific training and were given particular equipment in order to perform precise tactical roles on the battlefield. The French cavalry of the Napoleonic period was undoubtedly the strongest on the European continent, as was confirmed by Wellington on numerous occasions. Napoleon said that 'cavalry is useful before, during and after the battle'; this was particularly true for his own mounted regiments, which belonged to three main tactical categories and thus could perform a variety of different duties during a military engagement. The cavalry of the Grande Armée consisted of heavy cavalry, medium cavalry and light cavalry, each of which comprised two different categories of units: regiments of cuirassiers and carabiniers for the heavy cavalry, regiments of dragoons and lancers for the medium cavalry, and regiments of hussars and mounted chasseurs for the light cavalry. When Napoleon became First Consul of the French Republic in 1799, the French cavalry did not have regiments of lancers and its heavy cavalry were not equipped with cuirasses. As we will see, the emperor was a great cavalry reformer and introduced a series of innovations that improved the tactical flexibility of his mounted troops. Napoleon had a very clear vision of how to employ his cavalry on the battlefield. The heavy cavalry was tasked with conducting frontal charges during pitched battles, in order to use the power of its massive horses and its heavy equipment to break enemy infantry formations or rout their cavalry. The medium cavalry, meanwhile, was extremely versatile, being asked to both charge on the open field like the heavy cavalry but also to act as 'mounted infantry' and thus perform some duties that were typical of the line infantry (like defending positions). Finally, the light cavalry was designed to be used before and after the battle, conducting reconnaissance missions as well as pursuing fleeing enemies once they had been routed.

During the Revolutionary Wars, France's cavalry suffered greatly from the political changes that took place in French society and directly affected the army. Most of the pre-1789 cavalry officers were aristocrats from the most important noble families of France. These officers, however, following the implementing of the revolutionaries' reforms, left their units *en masse*, and thus a new officer corps for the mounted units had to be created almost from scratch. A great number of young and ambitious new officers rose from the rank-and-file in order to assume command of the cavalry corps. Among them were several capable individuals, who were promoted for their personal capabilities and not because they were rich aristocrats: these were the future marshals of the empire, including the likes of Murat, who would greatly improve the general quality of the French cavalry.

Napoleon had started his incredible military career as an artillery officer, and thus always paid special attention to the quality of this branch of the army, which he considered to be decisive for winning battles. The French artillery was the best in Europe before 1789, having been extensively reformed by the brilliant Lieutenant General Gribeauval from 1765 onwards. It was equipped with excellent guns and was very well trained, its officers possessing great technical competence and all being professional soldiers, not members of the aristocracy. Napoleon was the first military commander in history to use artillery in an offensive way, assembling hundreds of field pieces in 'grand batteries' that could hammer the enemy in preparation for frontal infantry attacks. The guns of the new Gribeauval system could be moved very rapidly, both on and off roads, this increased mobility favouring the development of horse artillery, which soon became an elite of the Napoleonic armies, despite having been created only a few years before Napoleon's rise to power.

In addition to the foot artillery and horse artillery, the technical units of the Grande Armée comprised various corps that only fought rarely on the battlefield but were fundamental to the success of the French Army. The engineers were the most important of these technical corps, providing highly specialized contingents of *sapeurs* (sappers), as well as a good number of competent officers who were capable of performing a huge variety of functions: they could conduct siege or counter-siege operations, build military or civil infrastructures such as bridges or camps, create field fortifications in a very short time and even establish new roads while the Grande Armée was on the march. The French engineers were completely independent logistically, having an autonomous baggage train that carried their tools and other materials and included talented artisans who could repair any kind of military infrastructure. They were supplemented by smaller units of auxiliary pioneers and a specialized corps of pontoniers (forming part of the artillery) that was capable of building solid bridges over all sizes of river. The artillery was further supplemented by several auxiliary corps, mostly of a static nature: the Coastal Artillery was tasked with garrisoning the many coastal fortifications of France; the Garrison Artillery was deployed in fortifications located away from the sea; the Veteran Artillery was made up of older gunners who could still perform static duties; the *ouvriers* were specialists in the construction and repair of guns and artillery carriages; and the *armuriers* could repair weapons of all types. The artillery also had its independent train, which moved the guns during campaigns and was responsible for transporting ammunition. The materials of the rest of the Grande Armée were assigned to an independent corps known as the *Train des Equipages* (Train of the Equipment), which was fully militarized by Napoleon.

Both the cavalry and technical corps of the French Army included a number of foreign units, each with very different backgrounds, which although often little known, made a significant contribution to French military success. The French Army under Napoleon conquered a large portion of Europe in just a few years, and in order to garrison all the newly occupied territories it needed the support of various paramilitary corps that sometimes played an important role during campaigns. The most important of these was the Gendarmerie, an ancient institution consisting of militarized policemen that was completely reformed during the Revolution. The Gendarmes not only kept order on the home front, but also patrolled the non-French territories conquered by Napoleon, such as the Iberian Peninsula, where they constantly fought against local insurgents known as *guerrilleros*. The city of Paris, the capital of the French Empire, had its own independent Municipal Guard that was autonomous from the Gendarmerie and even comprised a mounted branch. The French Navy of the Napoleonic period has often been considered a weak institution, and while this is partly true, it should be remembered that Napoleon never neglected it (especially during the early years of his reign when he planned to invade Britain). The French Navy comprised several corps that supported army units during land campaigns: Naval Infantry, Naval Artillery, Naval Engineers and Naval Artisans. These will all be covered in this book, since they had a lot in common with the land forces in terms of organization as well as their uniforms. In 1799, when Napoleon became First Consul of France, the French still controlled a significant colonial empire, comprising several territories. Some of these, such as Haiti on the island of Hispaniola in the Caribbean, were particularly flourishing and their agricultural production was important to the economy of France. Although Napoleon was never particularly interested in his colonies, to the point that he even sold Louisiana to the United States in 1803, he retained the services of a number of colonial military units that fought on several occasions during the Napoleonic Wars. The French colonial soldiers tried to crush the Haitian Revolution during the time of Napoleon's political rise as First Consul, and later attempted to preserve the independence of the territories they were garrisoning by repulsing frequent attacks mounted by the Royal Navy. In 1811, the French secured control of the extensive colonial possessions of the Netherlands, which led fighting in several further campaigns against the British. It should also be remembered that some minor colonial units (including a large number of foreigners) were also employed in Europe to perform auxiliary duties for the French.

Chapter 1

The Cuirassiers

History and organization

The cuirassiers first appeared in European armies during the second half of the sixteenth century, being created to replace the former fully armoured mounted men-at-arms, whose tactics and military traditions went back to the Middle Ages. The introduction of new and smaller firearms that could be discharged on horseback gradually led to pistols replacing the heavy lance as the main weapon of the cavalry. The new European heavy cavalrymen who dominated the battlefields of the Thirty Years War (1618–48) were mostly cuirassiers, non-aristocratic fighters armed with pistols and sword, and who no longer wore armour on their arms and legs. These horsemen soon became known as 'cuirassiers', since their armour was reduced to only the cuirass (originally consisting of both breastplate and backplate). By 1660, most of the European armies had modified the panoply of their heavy cavalry contingents: armoured helmets – which had been popular until that time – gradually faded from use, together with the backplate of the cuirass. In addition, pistols lost most of their importance, cuirassiers starting to be equipped only with a massive straight-bladed sword. Combat experience in the first half of the eighteenth century showed military commanders of many nations that the cuirasses of the heavy cavalry had lost most of its previous protective function, the new flintlock muskets of the infantry being easily able to pierce any kind of cuirass, even from quite a distance. Consequently, some armies, including those of the French, transformed their cuirassiers into line cavalry by abolishing the use of breastplates. There were, however, several significant exceptions to this rule: Frederick the Great of Prussia, for example, never deprived his heavy cavalry of cuirasses, which he thought could still be of great use during hand-to-hand cavalry combats.

By the outbreak of the French Revolution, several European armies – such as the Austrians and the Russians – still included units of cuirassiers, while others – for example the French and the British – did not prescribe the use of breastplates for their heavy cavalry regiments. Following the reorganization of 1793, the French cavalry comprised a total of twenty-five heavy regiments, that were commonly known as *cavalerie de ligne* or line cavalry. The troopers of these units did not have helmets

Officer of the cuirassiers wearing M1803 dress.

Troopers of the cuirassiers with M1803 dress. The figure on the left has the campaign breeches, while the one on the right wears the *bonnet de police* and the *surtout* (the latter is barely visible under the grey mantle that was used during winter).

or cuirasses, but were easily distinguishable from the rest of the French cavalrymen since they were armed with straight swords and wore tall leather boots. Traditionally, the heavy cavalry regiments had been officered by some of the most important members of France's aristocracy, so the political events of the French Revolution had a great impact on the command structure of these units, which lost their previous high morale. The proud regimental titles – which were based on well-established traditions – were abolished as the revolutionary government strove to eradicate the aristocratic character of the French heavy cavalry. During the Revolutionary Wars, the French line cavalry did not perform particularly well, its lack of cohesion and training apparent on several occasions. After becoming First Consul, Napoleon decided that his heavy cavalry had to be completely reformed to become much more effective on the battlefield. To achieve this, he had in mind to transform his line cavalrymen back into cuirassiers in order to distinguish them – from a tactical point of view – from the medium cavalry of the dragoons. Napoleon, like Frederick the Great, was convinced that having a number of mounted regiments equipped with metal cuirasses could give him a great advantage when fighting large-scale cavalry battles. Furthermore, he believed that cuirassiers could be employed as a 'shock force' that could break enemy infantry formations with well-planned and well-conducted frontal charges. For these reasons, in October 1801, the First Consul transformed the 1st Line Cavalry Regiment into the 1st Regiment of Cuirassiers, equipping them with helmets and breastplates. After a short experimentation with this single unit, Napoleon restructured his whole heavy cavalry in September 1802. Until that moment, each regiment of line cavalry had consisted of three squadrons. Napoleon ordered a reduction in regiments from twenty-five to eighteen, but increased the number of squadrons in each unit from three to four. Of the eighteen new heavy regiments, six were to be equipped with cuirasses. By the end of 1803, however, twelve of the new units had been given cuirasses and the remaining ones were deprived of their heavy cavalry status. As a result of this important reform, from 1803 onwards the core of the French heavy cavalry started to consist of a dozen cuirassier regiments, which were equipped with full cuirasses (including breastplate and backplate) and were also given helmets.

The staff of each regiment initially consisted of the following elements: one colonel, one major, two lieutenant-colonels, one quartermaster, one surgeon-major, one chaplain, two adjutants, one trumpet-major and five master-artisans. The four squadrons that made up a regiment were structured on two companies each, a single company comprising the following elements: one captain, one lieutenant, one second lieutenant, one senior staff sergeant, four junior staff sergeants, one fourrier, eight brigadiers, one trumpeter and eighty-two troopers. A single company consisted of

The Cuirassiers 5

Trooper (centre) and trumpeters (right and left) of the cuirassiers. The central figure has the new M1812 dress, while the musicians have their peculiar pre-1812 uniforms in regimental colour.

Cuirassier with M1812 uniform.

two troops and thus had a very flexible structure. In 1807, the composition of the regimental staff became as follows: one colonel, one major, two squadron commanders, two adjutant-majors, one paymaster-quartermaster, one surgeon-major, one assistant-major, two sub-assistant-majors, two adjutants, one trumpet-major, one veterinary surgeon and six artisans (the latter being cobblers, tailors, armourers and saddlers). In March 1807, the number of squadrons in each cuirassier regiment was increased from four to five.

Maintaining in service a unit of heavy cavalry equipped with helmets and cuirasses was extremely costly, so during the Napoleonic period the number of cuirassier regiments was never greatly expanded. However, in December 1807, by assembling together several detachments from existing regiments that had been deployed in southern France for the upcoming invasion of Spain, a new Régiment Provisorie de Grosse Cavalerie (Provisional Regiment of Heavy Cavalry) was formed. In 1808, after having absorbed a new Provisional Regiment of Heavy Cavalry that had been created in the meantime, the unit became the new 13th Regiment of Cuirassiers. A third Régiment Provisorie de Grosse Cavalerie came into existence in 1808, but this, unlike the other two formations, never became part of a permanent unit. In 1810, the Kingdom of Holland, ruled by Napoleon's brother, Louis, ceased to be an independent state and was absorbed into the French Empire. As a result, the best units of the disbanded Dutch Army became part of the French Army. Among these was the Dutch 2nd Regiment of Cuirassiers, which was transformed into the 14th Regiment of Cuirassiers of the French Army.

During the Napoleonic Wars, cuirassier units fought with great distinction on several occasions, participating in all the major pitched battles. They particularly distinguished themselves at the Battle of Eylau in February 1807 when – under command of Murat – one of their impressive frontal charges saved Napoleon from what could have been a bitter defeat against the Russians. During the Russian campaign of 1812, the French heavy cavalry conducted another impressive charge at the Battle of Borodino, one of the bloodiest clashes in the history of the Napoleonic Wars. With the first restoration of the Bourbons that followed Napoleon's initial abdication, the number of cuirassier regiments was reduced to twelve. During the Belgian campaign of 1815 that followed Napoleon's return from exile on Elba, the French heavy cavalry fought with desperate courage at Quatre Bras and especially at Waterloo; during the latter clash, it tried in vain to break the solid defensive squares of Wellington's infantry. The cuirassiers, commanded by Ney, charged several times against the British and their allies, but were always repulsed and suffered heavy casualties. Nevertheless, Wellington was greatly impressed by their courage, as were other officers who admired their perfect discipline and great horsemanship. After

Troopers (left) and officer (right) of the cuirassiers with M1812 dress.

the second restoration of the Bourbons, the cuirassiers continued to be an important component of the French Army until the Franco-Prussian War of 1870–71.

Uniforms and equipment

The helmet of the cuirassiers consisted of an iron cap surrounded by a black fur turban and surmounted by a copper crest. On the front it had a black visor with the external edge in copper, while on the left side was a copper fitting holding a red plume. On the frontal point of the crest was a black pompom surmounted by a tuft of the same colour. Over the crest was a black horsehair mane and the helmet had a copper chinscale held on each side by a copper disk decorated with a five-pointed star. The helmets of the officers had the pompom placed on the frontal point of the crest in copper rather than black wool. The helmets of the trumpeters had the tuft and the horsehair mane in white. The helmet of the French cuirassiers, in a strongly Neoclassical style, was extremely elegant but quite uncomfortable to wear.

Trooper of the cuirassiers with the *pokalem* and *surtout* introduced in 1812 for service dress.

The cuirass, the most distinctive element of the French heavy cavalry's equipment, was made of iron and was produced in three different models during the Napoleonic period. The first model, designed in 1802, was not very rounded and thus formed a blunt angle at the bottom. It had a total of thirty-four copper rivets that were driven into the edges of both the breastplate and the backplate. The cuirass was put on by first hooking the ends of its brass-scaled shoulder straps to spherical copper buttons that were riveted to the front of the breastplate. The two halves of the cuirass were then fastened together at the waist by means of a copper-buckled white leather belt that was secured to the back plate by twin copper rivets at each end. In 1806, a new model of cuirass was introduced, which differed from the previous one only in that the bottom of the breastplate was now rounded-off. In 1809, a third model of cuirass came into use, this version having a more rounded profile and being slightly shorter than the previous ones. The officers' cuirasses were decorated with a deeply engraved single line of laurel branches 3cm from the external edge. The engraved line was gilded like the scaled shoulder straps. The trumpeters did not wear cuirasses. Inside all the cuirasses was a padded garment known as a *fraise*, which was red with white external edging.

In 1803, soon after their formation, the French cuirassiers were given a tunic that was much shorter but very similar to the one that the line cavalry had been wearing. This was dark blue and single-breasted, and was known as a *habit-surtout*. The tunic had a collar, round cuffs, cuff flaps and turnbacks in the regimental colour; the collar and the cuff flaps were piped in dark blue, while the front of the *habit-surtout* and the vertical 'false' pockets on the back of the tails were also piped in the regimental colour. On the turnbacks there were decorative dark blue flaming grenades. The shoulder straps of the tunic were dark blue, with regimental colour piping. The buttons of the *habit-surtout* were all made of pewter and were stamped with the distinctive number of each regiment. In 1809, a new model of tunic came into use that had mid-thigh-length tails without pockets and turnbacks. The new *habit-surtout* was never particularly appreciated by the soldiers and was soon replaced in 1812 by a new one that was very short-skirted but had both turnbacks and vertical simulated pockets. The tunic introduced in 1812 marked the last change in the development of a *habit-surtout* that could be easily worn by cavalrymen in a cuirass. The officers' dress had the buttons and the flaming grenade patches in silver. As an alternative to the *habit-surtout*, for service dress, the cuirassiers could wear a simpler *surtout* without piping on the front. In 1812, a new model of this more plain *surtout* came into use, with red piping to the collar, cuffs and on the front, in addition to turnbacks of the same colour. The *surtout* was usually worn with a black bicorn or with the fatigue cap known as a *bonnet de police*, which was dark blue with white piping and frontal tassel, bearing on the front a flaming grenade embroidered in white. The *habit-surtout* always had red fringed epaulettes, which were silver and showed rank for officers. The NCOs' rank was shown by simple stripes of white cloth that were applied on the lower sleeves, while the years of service of both NCOs and rankers were shown by red inverted chevrons applied on the left upper sleeve. The trumpeters, who had no cuirass, wore a *habit-surtout* that was in the regimental colour and had additional stripes of white lace on the front, as well as on the collar and cuffs. Their epaulettes were also white. The dress regulations of 1812 tried to regularize the uniforms of the musicians, introducing a standard 'Imperial Livery' that was to be worn by all of them. This consisted of a dark green single-breasted jacket ornamented with stripes of lace having alternate yellow and green segments. The yellow segments were decorated with an interwoven dark green crowned 'N', while the dark green ones were decorated with an interwoven yellow imperial eagle.

On parade, all the cuirassiers wore deer-hide breeches, which on campaign were replaced by practical overalls that were made of linen and could be of different colours (varying from light grey to grey-brown). These were fastened by cloth-covered buttons placed down the length of the outer seams. The parade breeches of the officers were of chamois-hide and were usually replaced on service by dark blue linen breeches. The outfit of the cuirassiers was completed by their tall black leather 'grenadier boots' and their white gloves. The belt equipment of all ranks was white leather. The saddle-cloth consisted of a white half-shabraque made of sheepskin that was edged with small triangles of cloth in regimental colours, and a dark blue shabraque edged in white that had a white flaming grenade on the back corner.

From their creation, the cuirassiers were armed with heavy cavalry swords with a straight blade; these were of the 'Year IX' model from 1803–05 and the 'Year XI' model between 1806 and 1815. Until 1812, the French cuirassiers were equipped with a couple of flintlock pistols, which could be of the 'Year IX' or 'Year XIII' model. From 1812 onwards, they started to bear a 'Year XI' model flintlock musketoon (short-barrelled musket), which had its own bayonet. The ammunition for this weapon was carried on his back by each cavalryman in a black leather pouch, which was suspended on a white leather crossbelt. The musketoon was not given to officers and trumpeters, who were armed only with sword and pistols.

Trumpeter of the cuirassiers with pre-1812 uniform in regimental colour.

The Cuirassiers 13

Trumpeter of the cuirassiers with pre-1812 dress in regimental colour (yellow for this unit, the 7th Regiment of Cuirassiers).

Chapter 2

The Carabiniers

History and organization

Grenadiers emerged as a new type of European infantry during the second half of the seventeenth century when various armies started to employ hand-grenades as a new weapon. These could be thrown by infantrymen and were quite simple to produce, and proved to be of great use during siege operations and in pitched battles to destroy enemy field fortifications. In order to use the new weapon most effectively, the various infantry units of the European armies started to select the tallest and strongest men among their members, retraining them as grenadiers and teaching them how to use hand-grenades on the battlefield. When this development took place during the late seventeenth century, the dominant military power of Europe was France, whose 'Sun King' Louis XIV had at his disposal the most innovative military force of the age. The French Army was the first to introduce military uniforms in the modern sense of the term in 1660, and the first to create independent units of grenadiers within the infantry regiments. From 1667, four men in each French infantry regiment started to be trained as grenadiers, and in 1671 a company of grenadiers started to be included in each infantry battalion. During the following decades, grenadiers became the elite of the French infantry thanks to their superior training and discipline. As time progressed, the French innovations were adopted by other European armies, and thus grenadiers could be found practically everywhere on the continent. Many monarchs later transformed their units of grenadiers into elite corps with 'guard' status, this new category of heavy infantry becoming increasingly popular.

Louis XIV created a company of 250 horse grenadiers inside his large Royal Household in 1676. The new corps was formed by assembling together the best foot grenadiers from all the battalions of the French line infantry. Originally, the Horse Grenadiers of the Royal Guard were trained to act as a sort of mounted infantry: they moved on horseback but fought on foot like ordinary grenadiers. Over time, however, they were transformed into a heavy cavalry force tasked with charging the enemy in close formation, its use of hand-grenades consequently declining in importance.

The second half of the seventeenth century saw the development of another new troop type, the carabiniers, whose name derived from the main weapon that they used, a *carabine* (carbine). This, at least during the early decades of its existence, was nothing more than a shortened version of the infantry's flintlock musket that could be employed by cavalrymen firing from horseback. The French were the first in Europe to understand the potential of this new cavalry weapon, which could significantly augment the firepower of the mounted troops. Until that time, the cavalry corps of European armies had mostly been equipped with light firearms (flintlock pistols) that had quite a short range. The late seventeenth century saw a series of experiments dealing with the tactical role that the new carabiniers were to adopt, it eventually becoming clear that some elite cavalry armed with carbines could be extremely useful on the battlefield since they could support the other horsemen armed only with swords with an accurate fire comparable to that of the infantry. Initially, only two carabiniers were added to each company of light cavalry, but in 1691 each light cavalry regiment was ordered to have an entire company of carabiniers that was to act as its vanguard. In November 1693, following the French victory over a largely Anglo-Dutch army at the Battle of Neerwinden – that was mostly decided by the carabiniers – Louis XIV decided to create an autonomous unit of carabiniers inside his army: the Carabiniers du Roi (King's Carabiniers). These were formed by bringing together all the carabinier companies that already existed in the French Army, and was therefore a unit with a very large establishment, consisting of 100 companies with thirty men each. The companies were structured on five brigades, each of which consisted of four squadrons and was thus comparable to a standard cavalry regiment. The members of the Carabiniers du Roi were selected from the best elements of the French mounted units: they had to be at least 1.73 metres tall, unmarried and of good character. They were paid higher wages than the ordinary cavalry and soon became an elite force, one of the finest cavalry corps of the French Army. The carabiniers changed denomination several times during the eighteenth century, but were always commanded by a leading member of the royal family (usually the king's younger brother).

    The carabiniers eventually assumed the same character as the mounted grenadiers in terms of uniforms and tactical duties, starting to be employed as a standard heavy cavalry unit. Their peculiar weapon, the flintlock carbine, had been adopted by most of the French Army's mounted corps, and thus they had lost most of their original distinctive character (which had also happened to the mounted grenadiers). In 1776, to cut costs, the five brigades of carabiniers were reduced to a single regiment of eight squadrons, each having five officers and 145 troopers. The corps remained a very aristocratic unit and continued to have an elite status during the following years. The carabiniers were reorganized again in 1779, this time into two brigades with five squadrons each, a single squadron now consisting of six officers and 156 troopers.

In 1788, shortly before the outbreak of the French Revolution, the two brigades were transformed into regiments, having four squadrons each. The two regiments of carabiniers were always brigaded together and thus were practically inseparable, making up an elite force of 'shock' heavy cavalry which was to be used only during the most important pitched battles. After the revolution and the removal of King Louis XVI from power, the new republican authorities decided to disband the two regiments of carabiniers, which it was felt represented the power of the king and the aristocracy within the French Army. After further discussion, however, it became clear that it would have been counterproductive to disband some of the best mounted units that the country had its disposal, so the two corps continued to exist. They received the new denomination of Grenadiers of the Mounted Troops and were reorganized as regiments with two squadrons of two companies each. The years of the Revolutionary Wars were characterized by a series of incidents involving the carabiniers, who always remained strong supporters of the king and did not have a high opinion of the new republican authorities. The two regiments were on the verge of being disbanded on several occasions, particularly when all the aristocrats were expelled from the French Army following the execution of the king in January 1793. Nevertheless, the carabiniers were able to survive this difficult period, during which they also distinguished themselves during several pitched battles.

After becoming First Consul in 1799, Napoleon paid special attention to his regiments of carabiniers, appointing some of his relatives and his most loyal supporters as officers in the two units, while also distributing richly decorated swords as 'weapons of honour' to many carabiniers in order to secure their loyalty. After the proclamation of the French Empire, the carabiniers hoped that they could become part of the newly created Imperial Guard due to the support they were giving to the new political regime, as well as their traditional elite status. However, this proved not to be possible because the Imperial Guard already included a regiment of heavy cavalry with the same distinctive features as the carabiniers (the Regiment of Mounted Grenadiers). Yet despite never becoming part of Napoleon's Guard, the regiments of carabiniers continued to enjoy a higher military status than the cuirassier regiments of the French heavy cavalry.

From an organizational point of view, the carabiniers followed all the same changes that were progressively introduced for the cuirassiers. In August 1806, their two regiments were ordered to have four squadrons each, a single squadron being formed by two companies, then in March 1807, the number of squadrons was increased to five. The carabiniers fought with distinction against the Russians at the Battle of Friedland in June 1807, during which they charged with great determination. From the Revolutionary Wars onwards they were known as the 'Army's butchers' because

The Carabiniers 17

Carabinier with pre-1810 parade dress.

of the violence of their attacks, which were practically unstoppable. The carabiniers participated in the 1809 campaign that was fought against the Austrians and took part in the bloody Battle of Wagram in July that year, during which they suffered severe losses. Napoleon, understanding very well that it was extremely difficult to replace the fallen carabiniers with men of the same quality, decided to change the uniform and equipment of their two regiments after the events of Wagram. The massive bearskin that had been worn until then was replaced by a helmet, while the dark blue uniforms were substituted with new white ones and cuirasses were distributed to all members of the two regiments (which now lost their mounted grenadier character

Carabinier with pre-1810 campaign dress.

and practically became cuirassiers). After receiving their new uniform and new equipment (their muskets were replaced with musketoons), the carabinier regiments were also given a new internal structure, with just four squadrons. By 1811, the carabiniers had completed their transformation and were ready to participate in the

Officers of the carabiniers wearing their new M1810 uniforms. The figure on the left has the light blue mantle that was used during winter.

Carabinier with M1810 uniform.

following year's invasion of Russia, during which they fought with enormous courage at the Battle of Borodino in September 1812 before suffering heavy losses during the long retreat that marked Napoleon's defeat. By the end of the campaign, almost all the members of the two regiments were dead.

In the early months of 1813, Napoleon had to rebuild his army practically from scratch, using all the resources that were still at his disposal. The two regiments of carabiniers were reconstituted with an establishment of five squadrons each, but their quality was no longer comparable to that of pre-1812, most of the new members being inexperienced young recruits who had never seen the battlefield. During the German campaign of 1813, the carabiniers suffered further significant losses and had to be reorganized once again for the defence of France in 1814. They took part in several engagements during that campaign until Napoleon was forced to abdicate. With the first restoration of the Bourbons, the aristocratic status of the carabiniers was reintroduced and their regiments were restructured on four squadrons each. When the emperor returned from exile in 1815, the carabiniers were more than happy to join his cause and to renounce their new 'royal' status. But the long years of the Napoleonic campaigns had changed their nature forever, and they were no longer the feared veterans of old. The carabiniers charged with great determination alongside the cuirassiers during the Battle of Waterloo in the hope of breaking the squares of Wellington's infantry, but their efforts proved in vain. With Napoleon's permanent exile and the second restoration of the Bourbons, the number of carabinier regiments in the French Army was reduced from two to one. The elite heavy cavalrymen remained part of the French Army until 1871, having finally achieved their objective of becoming part of the Imperial Guard during the years of Napoleon III's 'Second Empire'.

Uniforms and equipment

The pre-1810 uniform of the carabiniers was very similar to that of the Imperial Guard's Mounted Grenadiers. Its most distinctive element was a massive black bearskin – 31.8cm tall – with white wool cords plaited into flounders and tasselled at each end. The top of the headgear, at the back, was covered with a round piece of red felt cloth decorated with a white cross. On the left side of the bearskin, attached to a tricolour cockade, there was a red plume (half red and half white for trumpeters). In full dress uniform, the carabiniers wore a dark blue *habit* coat, which had a dark blue standing collar piped in red and red round cuffs piped in dark blue. The frontal lapels of the coat were red, while the cuff flaps were red with dark blue piping for the 1st Regiment and dark blue with red piping for the 2nd Regiment. The turnbacks of the tails were red and had horizontal false pockets on the back, which were decorated with three buttons and red piping. All the buttons of the *habit* were of white metal and showed a flaming grenade badge, which was reproduced in dark blue on the turnbacks. In 1808, the colour of the flaming grenades embroidered on the turnbacks was changed to white. The shoulders of the tunic had red fringed epaulettes, a distinctive element of the grenadier units' dress, but these became white in 1808. While carrying out most duties, the full dress *habit* described above was replaced with a dark blue single-breasted *surtout*, which was cut away high on the stomach. This had a dark blue collar and cuffs piped in red, while its front was piped in red and its turnbacks were red with dark blue decorative flaming grenades. Underneath both the *habit* and the *surtout*, a white sleeved waistcoat was worn. Like with the cuirassiers, two types of breeches were issued to each carabinier: the first were made from off-white sheep leather and the second were made of canvas. The former were used on parade while the latter – being dark blue – were fastened from top to bottom up the sides with bone buttons (which were in common use on campaign). Trumpeters were dressed like the other carabiniers, but their uniform was in reversed colours: red with dark blue facings. In addition, they had white piping on the collar, cuffs and frontal lapels. The epaulettes of trumpeters were white. The outfit of the carabiniers was completed, as for the cuirassiers, by tall black leather boots and white leather gauntlet-like gloves. The epaulettes of officers were silver and showed their rank. The NCOs' rank was shown by simple stripes of white cloth that were applied on the lower sleeves, while the years of service of both NCOs and rankers were shown by red inverted chevrons on the left upper sleeve. The belt equipment of all ranks was white leather. The saddle-cloth consisted of a white half-shabraque made of sheepskin that was edged with small triangles of cloth in red, and a dark blue shabraque edged in white that had a white flaming grenade on the back corner. The carabiniers also had a fatigue cap known as a *bonnet de police*: this was dark blue with white piping and frontal tassel, and on the front it bore a flaming grenade embroidered in white.

The new cuirassier-style uniform introduced for the carabiniers in 1810 was extremely elegant and quite unusual among the other Napoleonic cavalry, since it was white. The helmet of the new uniform was made of yellow brass and was decorated with a frontal band in white metal, which ended at the bosses for the chinscale. These bosses were of a rayed sunburst design with a brass five-pointed star in the centre. The frontal band of the helmet was decorated with a brass crowned 'N' and was swept up into a point below the front of the crest, which was made of yellow brass. A narrow white metal band continued from behind the chinscale bosses around the rear base of the skull. The rear neck guard of the helmet had an edging made of white metal. The crest was decorated with fluting and was surmounted by a large red 'caterpillar' of padded horsehair. The chinscale consisted of sixteen rows of white metal. The steel cuirass, much heavier and more costly than that of the cuirassiers, had a yellow brass plate soldered to its external surfaces but left a 25mm bare steel border all around, which was embellished with brass rivets. The breastplate and the backplate were held together by a belt of natural leather with a brass buckle, and by two shoulder straps that were covered with brass scales (these terminated in brass plates pierced with two fixing holes for studs). The inside of the cuirass was padded with a *fraise* of light blue cloth which had white external edging. As was the case with the cuirassiers, the *fraise* protruted above, below and in the armholes of the cuirass. The helmets and cuirasses of the officers were of a redder and more copper-rich alloy than those of

The Carabiniers

Carabinier with M1810 dress.

Carabinier wearing the M1810 uniform without cuirass.

the troopers, and also had silvered furniture. The officers' breastplates bore a silver rayed sunburst decoration on the front, which had a five-pointed star in the centre. Under the cuirass, a short-tailed and single-breasted white jacket was worn, which had a standing collar and round cuffs in light blue with white piping. The front edge of the jacket was piped in light blue, and the short tails had light blue turnbacks decorated with white flaming grenade badges. On the back of the tails were vertical false pockets with light blue piping and three buttons. The epaulettes worn on the shoulders were red with a white braid edging all round the top of their strap. The two regiments, like with the previous uniform, were distinguishable only by the colour of their cuff flaps; these were white with light blue piping for the 1st Regiment and light blue with white piping for the 2nd Regiment. The breeches remained the same, the campaign ones now being brown or grey. The trumpeters did not have the cuirass and wore a jacket with reversed colours (light blue with white facings), with white piping on collar and cuffs. The trumpeters' epaulettes were white, like the caterpillar of their helmets. The epaulettes of the officers were silver and showed their rank. The NCOs' rank was shown by simple stripes of white cloth applied on the lower sleeves, while the years of service of both NCOs and rankers were shown by red inverted chevrons on the left upper sleeve. The black leather boots, white leather gloves and white leather belt equipment remained unchanged. The saddle-cloth consisted of a white sheepskin half-shabraque edged with small triangles of cloth in light blue, plus a light blue shabraque edged in white that had a white flaming grenade on the back corner. The new dress regulations of 1812 tried to regularize the uniforms of the musicians, introducing a standard Imperial Livery to be worn by them all. This consisted of a dark green single-breasted jacket ornamented with stripes of lace with alternate yellow and green segments. The yellow segments were decorated with an interwoven dark green crowned 'N', while the dark green ones had an interwoven yellow Imperial Eagle.

Until 1810, the carabiniers were armed with heavy cavalry swords of the 'Year IV' and 'Year XI' model, which had a flaming grenade device stamped on their guard. They also carried a couple of 'Year IX' or 'Year XIII' flintlock pistols and a dragoon-style flintlock musket of the 'Year IX' or 'Year XIII' model. In 1810, the carabiniers replaced their straight swords with slightly curved sabres and their muskets with a cavalry musketoon of the 'Year IX' model.

Trumpeter of the carabiniers wearing M1810 dress.

Trumpeter of the carabiniers with M1812 uniform ('Imperial Livery').

Chapter 3

The Dragoons

History and organization

The first units of dragoons appeared in the European armies during the last phase of the Thirty Years War, the bloody conflict that ravaged most of present-day Germany between 1618 and 1648. The basic idea behind the formation of the first dragoon corps was to have some soldiers who could move on horseback but fight on foot. The armies of the time increasingly needed highly mobile troops that could travel long distances in a short time, but could also fight as standard infantry when needed. As a result, the first companies of dragoons were organized, consisting of ordinary infantrymen who knew how to ride a horse and could therefore perform as a sort of mounted infantry. The term 'dragoons' derived from the multi-tasked nature of these new soldiers: like the mythical beasts which gave them their name, capable of living on earth as well as on water, the dragoons could be employed as infantrymen but also as cavalry. One of the first armies to include these new soldiers in large numbers was the French one of Louis XIV, which already had two independent regiments of dragoons by 1660. Initially, these new corps had much more in common with the infantry than the cavalry: they did not wear boots like the ordinary mounted troops, they were organized in companies rather than in squadrons, their musicians were drummers and not trumpeters, and their main weapon was an infantry musket as opposed to a cavalry sword.

During the eighteenth century, the dragoons partially changed their nature, only very rarely being employed as mounted infantry. On most occasions they were asked to act as regular cavalry, being tasked with conducting frontal charges and other tactical functions that were typical of the mounted 'shock' troops. The dragoons gradually became a sort of medium cavalry: they had lighter equipment than the heavy cavalry cuirassiers, but heavier equipment than the light horsemen. Consequently, a dragoon unit could attack the enemy with a frontal charge but could also conduct skirmishing operations in open order. Only in France did the dragoons retain part of their original mounted infantry function, differently from in other European countries. Indeed, the French Army's dragoons were equipped with bayonets and could fight dismounted if needed. Napoleon continued this French tradition, and during his reign he frequently employed his dragoons as normal infantrymen. In 1786, the French regiments of dragoons were given a distinctive new uniform comprising a helmet and dark green coat. Although this was modified several times during the following decades, its basic elements remained the same until 1871. The green colour of the coat became so strongly associated with the dragoons that it soon started to be known as 'dragoon green'. There were twenty-four regiments of dragoons in the French Army in 1786, but this number was reduced to eighteen two years later when the royal government decided to create a new corps of mounted chasseurs, converting six of the existing dragoon units into this new role. In 1793, the new republican government increased the number of dragoon regiments to twenty-one.

Napoleon, who appreciated the tactical flexibility of his dragoons and liked to employ them as infantry when needed, decided to augment the number of dragoon units in his armies soon after becoming First Consul. In 1803, nine new regiments of dragoons were created, bringing the total number to thirty, a number which would remain stable until 1811, when six dragoon regiments were converted into lancer units (see the following chapter for details). Of the new regiments of dragoons that were formed by Napoleon in 1803, six were former units of line cavalry and three had been units of hussars. According to the organization prescribed in September 1803, each regiment of dragoons was to be structured on four squadrons and each squadron was to consist of two companies. The staff of each regiment comprised the following elements: one colonel, one major, two squadron commanders, one adjutant sub-officer, one staff sergeant, one brigadier-trumpeter, one brigadier-drummer, one brigadier-sapper and eight sappers. The small squad of sappers that was part of the regimental staff had a very important function, being tasked with clearing the way for its unit during marches and with building field fortifications.

The mixed infantry/cavalry nature of the dragoon regiments was recognizable in the presence of some sappers in each regimental staff, but also in the internal structure of each company. According to the organization introduced in 1803, a company of dragoons consisted of the following elements: one captain, one lieutenant, two sub-lieutenants, one brigadier-fourrier, four brigadiers (corporals), one trumpeter, one drummer, fifty-four mounted rankers and thirty-six dismounted rankers. As this makes clear, each company of dragoons was a mixed unit of foot and horse, there being a trumpeter for the mounted rankers and a drummer for the foot rankers. The composition of the regimental staff changed very little during between 1803 and 1811, apart from the abolition of the staff sergeant in 1808. In 1811, one quartermaster, two adjutant-majors and one major-surgeon were added to each regimental staff. In 1807, after having fought with great distinction during several campaigns, all the French dragoons were given horses and their peculiar mixed nature of infantry and

Officer of the dragoons with pre-1812 dress.

Foot dragoons charging in 1805.

cavalry was lost. From 1803–06, Napoleon experimented a lot with the tactics to be employed by his dragoons. In the event of mobilization for war, the foot soldiers of the various dragoon regiments were detached from their parent units and were assembled into temporary foot brigades. At the camp at Boulogne that was built in preparation for the planned invasion of Great Britain in 1803, the foot dragoons were assembled into five foot brigades (each of which was formed by the foot dragoons provided by three or four regiments). For the campaign of 1805 that culminated with victory over the Russians and Austrians at the Battle of Austerlitz, the foot dragoons were instead assembled into four temporary regiments with two battalions each. Another independent battalion of foot dragoons was organized – still in 1805 – for the French military forces fighting against the Austrians in northern Italy. Finally, for the Prussian campaign of 1806, another two temporary regiments of foot dragoons were created, with two battalions in each.

Dragoon officer of a standard company (left), dragoon officer of an elite company (centre, with bearskin) and dragoon sapper (right, with bearskin).

Dragoons of the 17th Regiment with M1812 uniform.

Napoleon was not particularly enthusiastic about his dismounted dragoons' combat performance and so – after having captured enough horses from his enemies – decided to end all his tactical experiments and to give mounts to all his dragoons. While his provisional units of foot dragoons were a disappointment for the emperor, the mounted ones fought very well during several important pitched battles, including Austerlitz and Jena. From 1807 onwards, the dragoons distinguished themselves in all the major battles fought by French armies, such as Eylau, Friedland

and Wagram. The dragoons made a great contribution to Napoleon's war efforts in Spain, where they countered the local insurgents (*guerrilleros*) very effectively thanks to their mixed cavalry/infantry training. The Russian campaign of 1812 and German campaign of 1813 had a terrible impact on the dragoon regiments, many of which were completely destroyed. Napoleon was able to completely rebuild his dragoon units after these setbacks, but only with young recruits who had very little combat experience. Following the first restoration of the Bourbons, the number of dragoon regiments in the French Army was reduced to fifteen, many of which participated in the Belgian campaign of 1815 that culminated in Napoleon's final defeat at Waterloo.

Uniforms and equipment

The distinctive headgear of the dragoons was an elegant helmet in Neoclassical style, known as the *Casque à la Minerve* (Minerva Helmet) since it resembled the mythical headgear worn by the ancient Roman goddess. It was made of a yellow alloy very similar to copper and was encircled by a brown fur turban. On the helmet's cap was a heavily embossed copper crest supporting a black horsehair mane, while on the front of the headgear there was a black leather peak that could have a copper external edge. The chinstrap of the helmet could be of black leather or be covered with copper scales, attached on each side of the headgear to a copper disk decorated with a five-pointed star. The turban could be pointed at the front and could have two stripes of copper on the external edges. On the frontal point of the crest, on top of a copper pompom, there was a small tuft made of black wool. On parade, a plume was inserted in a copper holder that was placed just forward of the left-hand chinstrap disk. The plume was white for most of the regiments, but its colour varied from unit to unit (red and green being quite popular). The 1812 dress regulations, in trying to regularize the use of plumes, prescribed that they had to be replaced with simple discs of cloth. These had to be in a particular colour for each squadron: red for the 1st Squadron, sky blue for the 2nd, orange for the 3rd and violet for the 4th. This scheme of colours had to be adopted by each regiment for all its squadrons. The gradual substitution of the plumes with discs took place very slowly, and even in 1814 it was not uncommon to see dragoon helmets with coloured plumes.

According to a decree issued by Napoleon on 10 October 1801, the 1st Company of the 1st Squadron of each dragoon regiment was to be known as the Elite Company, since its members were the most experienced veterans of their unit. These soldiers, in order to be distinguished from the others, had the privilege of wearing a distinctive headgear: a massive black bearskin – almost 32cm tall – with red wool cords plaited into flounders and tasselled at each end. The top of the headgear, at the back, was

The Dragoons 35

Dragoon of the 4th Regiment wearing the *surtout* that was used until 1812.

covered with a round piece of red felt cloth decorated with a white cross. On the left side of the bearskin, attached to a tricolour cockade, was a red plume. The soldiers of the Elite Company, in grenadier tradition, also had red fringed epaulettes that distinguished them from the ordinary dragoons. The few sappers that were attached to each regiment of dragoons wore the same peculiar distinctions as the Elite Company. They used the bearskin as headgear and wore the red epaulettes; in addition, they

Sapper of the 1st Regiment of Dragoons with pre-1812 dress.

had a specific badge consisting of two crossed axes embroidered in red on the upper sleeves and wore a white leather apron. Their specific equipment included a massive axe and the white leather crossbelt holding their ammunition pouch had a distinctive brass badge on the front (consisting of a flaming grenade above two crossed axes).

The bearskin of the Elite Company and sappers could have a brass flaming grenade on the front or could be replaced with a smaller 'light cavalry' busby, having its same main features. The trumpeters used the same headgear as the ordinary dragoons, but with white horsehair mane and white tuft; on parade they wore plumes that were white in the bottom half and in regimental colour in the upper half. The trumpeter of the Elite Company could have a white bearskin instead of the usual black one.

With service/campaign dress, the helmet and bearskin were usually replaced by the *bonnet de police* fatigue cap. This, like for all the units of the French Army, comprised a turban and a '*flamme*' (flame; a decorative strip of cloth) that were dark green for the dragoons. The uppermost edge of the turban was piped in white, while the *flamme* was piped in the regimental colour and ended in a white tassel. The front of the cap bore a flaming grenade badge embroidered in white or in regimental colour. The dress regulations of 1812 introduced a new model of fatigue cap known as the *pokalem*, which had the same colour and basic features of the *bonnet de police* but consisted of a large and round turban with a flat top and ear flaps. The *pokalem*, according to the official dress regulations, was to replace the *bonnet de police* as the fatigue cap of both the heavy and medium cavalry, yet in practice it was used only sporadically as the *bonnet de police* continued to be worn after 1812.

With full dress, the dragoons wore a dark green *habit* coat, which had a standing collar and round cuffs in regimental colour. The frontal lapels of the coat were in the regimental colour, while the cuff flaps were dark green with piping in regimental colour. The turnbacks of the tails were in regimental colour, with vertical or horizontal false pockets on the back, which were decorated with three buttons and with piping in regimental colours. All the buttons of the *habit* were made of pewter and were embossed with the distinctive number of each regiment. The coat had dark green shoulder straps piped in regimental colour. On the turnbacks were decorative flaming grenade badges embroidered in dark green. The areas of the coat in regimental colour, their position and the direction of the false pockets on the tails (vertical or horizontal) distinguished the various regiments. Wherever the facings were of one of the many distinctive colours, they were piped in dark green; when their regimental colour was dark green, they were piped in a secondary regimental colour. From 1799–1812, the general cut of the dragoons' *habit* changed only very slightly, becoming slimmer and shorter; its turnbacks, for example, became false and stitched along their entire length. The illusion of true turnbacks was initially maintained by the retention of the triangle of dark green cloth visible beneath their juncture, but by 1810 this practice had ceased. Under the *habit*, a simple white waistcoat was worn, which had twin pockets at the waist and a single row of buttons on the front.

For most duties, the full dress *habit* described above was replaced with a dark green single-breasted *surtout*, which was cut away high on the stomach. This had dark green collar and cuffs piped in regimental colour, its front also piped in regimental colour while its turnbacks were in regimental colour with dark green decorative flaming grenades. The new dress regulations issued on 8 February 1812 prescribed the abolition of the old-fashioned *habit* and the introduction of the new *habit-veste*. This differed from the previous coat in being fastened to the waist and having a

Sapper of the 7th Regiment of Dragoons with pre-1812 uniform and busby.

Sapper of the 30th Regiment of Dragoons wearing pre-1812 dress and bearskin.

considerably shorter skirt. In addition, the frontal lapels that were present on the former *habit* were united to form a single frontal plastron on the *habit-veste*. The latter retained all the colours and basic features of the old coat. The new regulations also prescribed that the existing model of white waistcoat be replaced with a new one having a round-fronted shape (which was to be invisible beneath the *habit-veste*). Two types of breeches were issued to each dragoon: the first were made of off-white coarse hide and the second of canvas. The former were used on parade, while the latter – being in various shades of grey and brown – were fastened from top to bottom up the sides with bone buttons. The trumpeters of the dragoon regiments wore a *habit* in reversed colours, i.e. they were dressed in regimental colour with dark green facings. The musicians' dress had white piping on collar, cuffs and frontal lapels. The epaulettes of the trumpeters were white. The dress regulations of 1812 regularized the uniforms of the musicians, with a standard Imperial Livery worn by

Sapper of the 19th Regiment of Dragoons wearing M1812 uniform and busby.

The Dragoons 41

Dragoon trumpeter with pre-1812 dress in regimental colour.

all of them. This consisted of a dark green single-breasted jacket ornamented with stripes of lace having alternate yellow and green segments. The yellow segments were decorated with an interwoven dark green crowned 'N', while the dark green ones were decorated with an interwoven yellow imperial eagle. The outfit of the dragoons was completed by tall black leather boots and white leather gauntlet-like gloves. The epaulettes of officers were silver and showed their rank, the NCOs' rank being shown by simple stripes of white cloth applied on the lower sleeves, while the years of service of both NCOs and rankers were indicated by red inverted chevrons on the left upper sleeve. The belt equipment of all ranks was white leather. The saddle-cloth consisted of a white half-shabraque made of sheepskin that was edged with small triangles of cloth in regimental colours, plus a dark green shabraque edged in white that had a white regimental number on the back corner.

Until 1804, the French dragoons were equipped with the same M1777 Charleville musket that was issued to the line infantry, but thereafter they received the new cavalry musketoon of the 'Year IX' model that was designed specifically for them. This was later produced in a slightly improved version, known as the 'Year XI' model. Both the early musket and the musketoon could have a bayonet attached. Each dragoon also had a couple of flintlock pistols, which could be of the 'Year IX' or 'Year XIII' model. Prior to 1804, the swords of the dragoons were of the heavy 'Year IV' model, which was replaced successively by the newer 'Year IX', 'Year XI' and 'Year XII' models. These swords gradually became the definitive weapon of the dragoons.

Chapter 4

The Lancers

History and organization

By the outbreak of the French Revolution, three of the major European armies included some units of medium cavalry equipped with lances: the Russian Army, the Austrian Army and the Prussian Army. Since the second half of the sixteenth century, Poland had been the homeland of a new kind of cavalry armed with lances, whose members were known as 'uhlans' and soon became the national cavalry of the Polish state, like the hussars (as we will see in the following chapter) were the national cavalry of Hungary. The Polish uhlans were extremely versatile and flexible tactically: being lightly equipped, they could act as explorers or skirmishers; being armed with lances, they could also charge against enemy infantry or fight large cavalry battles. The Polish lancers became famous for their mastery in the use of the lance, which gave them a great advantage over enemy horsemen who were armed only with swords or sabres. A Polish uhlan could kill his cavalry opponent from a distance by using a weapon that was both simple and cheap to produce compared with a sword or sabre. During the second half of the eighteenth century, the Polish state was partitioned between the three major military powers of eastern Europe – Russia, Austria and Prussia – and had ceased to be an autonomous political entity by 1795. The Russians, Austrians and Prussians then started to recruit some units of lancers from their new Polish subjects. These corps had their baptism of fire during the Revolutionary Wars and performed well in battle on several occasions.

Meanwhile, the French also organized their own units of lancers, recruiting large numbers of Polish political exiles who had decided to continue the struggle for the freedom of their country by joining the French armed forces. Napoleon had a great admiration for his Polish cavalry and their combat abilities, but for several years he refrained from creating new lancer units made up of French horsemen since he considered them to be incapable of performing the same tactical duties as the Polish cavalry. During the Polish campaign of 1807 against Russia, however, Napoleon realized that horsemen equipped with lances had enormous potential on the battlefield, having observed the actions of the Russian lancer units. Russia, unlike Austria and Prussia, did not restrict itself to only a few units of lancers recruited from its Polish territories, but also deployed massive numbers of semi-regular lancers recruited from the Cossacks or the nomadic peoples living in its Asian possessions. The Cossacks were without doubt among the best light cavalrymen who fought in the Napoleonic Wars: they were ferocious, fast-moving and incredibly effective. Riding small horses, they could move very rapidly on every kind of terrain and were able to launch surprise attacks against any kind of enemy force. They were excellent skirmishers and skilled explorers, but when needed they could also pursue a routed enemy or launch frontal charges against other cavalry. Their mastery in the use of the

Officer of the 1st Regiment of Lancers.

Trooper of the Elite Company, 1st Regiment of Lancers.

lance was absolute, making them more than a match for all opponents. Napoleon was greatly impressed by the capabilities of the Cossacks, witnessing that his traditional cavalry units were unable to face them on the battlefield on equal terms. As a result, after some years of experimentations, he decided that some entirely 'national' units of lancers must be created within the French Army for future confrontations with the Cossacks. The lancer regiments of the Grande Armée were organized in 1811, and when a year later the French Army invaded Russia and they had to face hordes of Cossacks. The Cossacks' effective and violent attacks against his troops, together with the harsh weather conditions, were key factors behind Napoleon's Russian disaster. Indeed, during the long retreat from Moscow, the survivors of the French Army were constantly harassed by Cossack light cavalry and suffered heavy casualties due to the hit-and-run tactics employed by the Russian mounted skirmishers. The defeat suffered in Russia convinced Napoleon that the Cossacks were the best cavalry deployed by his enemies, so during the last years of his rule, the emperor continued to sponsor the formation of new lancer units in the French Army. During the campaigns of 1813 and 1814, the Cossacks played a prominent role, showing their superiority over their French opponents on several occasions. After having followed the French all the way from Moscow, they finally entered Paris on their small but study horses in the summer of 1814.

The lancers of the French Army were created through an Imperial Decree on 18 June 1811, being given the official denomination of Chevau-Légers Lanciers (Light Cavalry Lancers). There were nine regiments of lancers, which were not brand new units but converted formations that were already in existence. The 1st Regiment of Lancers was the former 1st Regiment of Dragoons, the 2nd Regiment of Lancers had been the 3rd Regiment of Dragoons, the 3rd Regiment of Lancers was the old 8th Regiment of Dragoons, the 4th Regiment of Lancers comprised the former 9th Regiment of Dragoons, the 5th Regiment of Lancers was the former 10th Regiment of Dragoons, the 6th Regiment of Lancers was made up from the 29th Regiment of Dragoons, the 7th Regiment of Lancers was the former 1st Lancer Regiment of the Vistula Legion, the 8th Regiment of Lancers had previously been the 2nd Lancer Regiment of the Vistula Legion and the 9th Regiment of Lancers was the old 30th Regiment of Mounted Chasseurs. Most of the new lancer corps were thus formed by converting dragoon units, so the links between the dragoons and lancers were always very strong. The 30th Regiment of Mounted Chasseurs had a very peculiar history, being mostly made up of German soldiers and created only in February 1811, just a few months before becoming a lancer corps. The regiment was formed by assembling together the German cavalrymen of the Hanoverian Legion (see Chapter 12 for more details on this corps) and a dragoon regiment raised by the independent city of Hamburg. The two regiments from the Polish Vistula Legion were already equipped with lances and had an excellent military reputation (for more details about their early history, see Chapter 12). At the Battle of Albuera in May 1811, they routed an entire brigade of British infantry and captured several enemy guns.

To give some proper training in the use of the cavalry lance to his new lancer regiments, Napoleon ordered the most experienced members of the Vistula Legion's cavalry and the Imperial Guard's Polish Lancers to act as instructors for the new units of Chevau-Légers Lanciers. Having completed their intensive training, the lancer regiments soon became one of the most important components of the Napoleon's cavalry. They fought with great determination during the Russian campaign – which was their first taste of battle – launching effective counter-attacks against

NCO of the 5th Regiment of Lancers, wearing the frontal plastron of his uniform buttoned across to show its dark green side.

the Cossacks. They also served with valour during the campaigns of 1813 and 1814 which ended with the fall of France and the abdication of the emperor. Under the first restoration of the Bourbons, the number of lancer regiments was reduced to six, the three 'foreign' units being disbanded. After Napoleon's return to France, the

48 Napoleon's Cavalry, Artillery and Technical Corps 1799–1815

Trooper (left), trumpeter (centre) and officer (right) of the 1st Regiment of Lancers.

lancer regiments participated with distinction at the Battle of Waterloo, launching a deadly counter-attack that almost annihilated Wellington's Royal Scots Greys. With the end of the Napoleonic Wars, the lancers remained a stable component of the French medium cavalry for many years, and the British – who had admired them at Waterloo – also introduced lancer units to their mounted corps.

The internal organization of the French lancer regiments was almost the same as that of the dragoons, which has been described in the previous chapter. Each company consisted of a first rank equipped with lances and a second rank equipped only with sabres. The first rank comprised of two sergeants, four corporals and forty-four troopers, while the second rank had four corporals and forty-four troopers. These were supplemented by various supernumerary elements, who were not part of either of the ranks: one sergeant-major, two sergeants, three fourriers, two trumpeters and eighteen troopers (half of them equipped with lances, half with carbines). In total, only half of the horsemen were armed with lances in each company. The composition of the regimental staff was exactly the same as the dragoon units, and each regiment comprised four squadrons with two companies each. The 1st Company of the 1st Squadron, like in the dragoon regiments, was known as the Elite Company.

Uniforms and equipment

The uniform assigned to the new regiments of lancers in 1811 derived from that used by the dragoons and thus retained many similar features, especially to the one introduced in 1812, which had a frontal plastron instead of the old-fashioned lapels. The headgear of the lancers was no more than a modified version of the dragoon helmet. Where the dragoon helmet's copper crest bore a horsehair mane, the lancer's helmet supported a Neoclassical black horsehair crest; and while the rear of the dragoon helmet's copper cap was simply rounded, the lancer's helmet had a rear peak that was introduced to protect the back of the neck from cuts and rain. The plume added to the headgear on parade, like for the dragoons, could be of several colours, which varied according to the regiment. Most of the lancer units, however, had a plume that was red or white. When the 1812 dress regulations prohibited the use of plumes, the lancers simply removed them from their helmets and did not replace them with the coloured discs of cloth that were officially prescribed. The fatigue cap worn on service/campaign was identical to that of the dragoons, but instead of a flaming grenade on the front it bore two crossed lances. In 1812, the lancers also received the new dark green *pokalem*, always with two crossed lances embroidered in their regimental colour on the front. The soldiers of the elite company wore the same helmet as the other troopers, but with the horsehair crest in red. In addition, they also had red fringed epaulettes. The regiments of lancers, differently from those of dragoons, did not include any sappers in their regimental staff. The trumpeters used the same headgear as the ordinary lancers, but with white crest and plume.

Trooper and officer of the 9th Regiment of Lancers (left), and officer and trooper of the 7th Regiment of Lancers (right).

With full dress, the lancers wore a dark green *habit-veste* coat, which had standing collar and pointed cuffs in regimental colour. The frontal plastron of the coat was in regimental colour, and the pointed cuffs had no cuff flaps. The frontal plastron of the *habit-veste* was reversible and thus could be either buttoned back (to reveal the

The Lancers

Trumpeter of the 2nd Regiment of Lancers (left) and trumpeter of the 1st Regiment of Lancers (right).

facing colour) or buttoned across (to show its dark green side plus a narrow strip in regimental colour). The turnbacks of the short tails were in regimental colours like the other facings: scarlet red for the 1st Regiment, orange for the 2nd Regiment, pink for the 3rd Regiment, crimson red for the 4th Regiment, sky blue for the 5th Regiment and brighter red for the 6th Regiment. The last three regiments of lancers (the 7th, 8th and 9th) had their own distinctive uniforms that will be described below. The turnbacks of the *habit-veste* were supposed to be decorated with dark green badges reproducing an imperial eagle, but such badges were only rarely found on the actual uniforms. The buttons of the coat were of yellow metal. A sleeveless and round-edged white waistcoat was worn beneath the *habit-veste*, being practically impossible to see. For most types of duties the full dress *habit-veste* described above was replaced with a dark green single-breasted shell-jacket, which had piping in regimental colour on the front and on the facings. Trumpeters wore the same *habit-veste* as the ordinary lancers, but with white epaulettes and white piping to collar, cuffs and frontal plastron. In addition, they had decorative stripes of golden lace on the sleeves and on the front of their coat (which was single-breasted and thus did not have the standard frontal plastron). The dress regulations of 1812 that regularized the uniforms of the musicians introduced the standard Imperial Livery, which was also prescribed for the trumpeters of the dragoon regiments. All the lancers wore dark green 'Hungarian breeches' on parade, which were laced down the outer leg and the edges of the front flaps in yellow. The ornament of the flaps consisted of an inverted arrowhead device for the regiments numbered 1–4 and a more complicated 'Hungarian knot' for those numbered 5–6. On campaign, dark green overalls, reinforced with black leather on the inside, were in general use, with side-stripes in regimental colours and yellow metal buttons applied down the outer leg. Later, especially after the Russian campaign, overalls of different colours (notably grey) became increasingly popular. The outfit of the lancers was completed by black leather Hussar-style boots with yellow top piping and frontal tassel, as well as by white leather gauntlet-like gloves. The epaulettes of officers were golden and showed their rank. The NCOs' rank was shown by simple stripes of yellow cloth that were applied on the lower sleeves, while the years of service of both NCOs and rankers were shown by red inverted chevrons on the left upper sleeve. The belt equipment of all ranks was white leather. The saddle-cloth comprised a white sheepskin half-shabraque that was edged with small triangles of cloth in regimental colour, and a dark green shabraque edged in yellow that had a yellow regimental number on the back corner.

The main weapon of the lancers was a 2.75-metre-long lance, which had a shaft made of hardwood (such as ash) and a point of steel. The bottom of the lance had

The Lancers 53

Trumpeter of the 1st Regiment of Lancers wearing the new 'Imperial Livery' introduced in 1812.

a steel 'shoe' to protect the wood of the shaft when the weapon was rested on the ground. The centre of the shaft had a whitened leather grip and a loop for the fingers known as a *martingale*. The point was made with a flattened diamond-shaped section that allowed easier penetration and was secured by long steel straps that made it harder to chop off with a sword or sabre. The lance was decorated with a Polish-style red-and-white pennon. In addition to the lance, the lancers also carried a flintlock musketoon of the 'Year IX' model, a light cavalry sabre of the 'Year IX' model and a couple of 'Year IX' or 'Year XIII' model flintlock pistols.

The regiments numbered 7–9 had the same equipment as the other ones, but wore peculiar uniforms. The two units that had previously been part of the Vistula Legion were dressed in perfect Polish style, with a dark blue *czapka* with squared top piped in white on the edges and on the front, tricolour French cockade, white cords and flounders, brass frontal plate including a central part in white metal bearing a letter 'N', black bottom band, black peak edged in brass, brass chinscale and black plume with point in regimental colour (yellow for the 7th Regiment, red for the 8th Regiment). They also wore a dark blue *kurtka* with standing collar, pointed cuffs, frontal plastron and short turnbacks in regimental colour, plus white epaulettes and white aiguillettes on the left shoulder. They had dark blue trousers with double side-stripes in regimental colour, black leather boots and white belt equipment. The shabraque was dark blue with external edging in the regimental colour. The uniform of the 9th Regiment of Lancers, formerly the 30th Regiment of Mounted Chasseurs, included a red *czapka* with squared top piped in white on the edges and on the front, tricolour French cockade, white cords and flounders, brass frontal plate including a central part in white metal with a letter 'N', black bottom band, black peak edged in brass, brass chinscale and yellow short plume. Their dark green *kurtka* had a standing collar, pointed cuffs, frontal plastron and short turnbacks in yellow, with dark green shoulder straps piped in yellow. They also wore red trousers with large side-stripes in dark green, black leather boots and white belt equipment, while the shabraque was red with external edging in dark green.

Chapter 5

The Hussars

History and organization

During the opening decades of the eighteenth century, the heavy cavalry were the most important European mounted troops, making up the bulk of the cavalry forces mobilized by various nations and having progressively acquired tactical supremacy on the continent's battlefields. Highly trained and well disciplined, the heavy cavalry consisted of horsemen armed with long swords having straight blades and mounted on massive horses, able to charge and manoeuvre in perfect order by maintaining 'knee-to-knee' close formations. These cavalry were mostly employed to conduct frontal charges and to cover the retreat of line infantry when they were routed by the enemy. Since the Thirty Years War, cavalry had started to perform a series of auxiliary roles for the infantry and were rarely used in an autonomous way. There were, however, some exceptions to this general rule. In eastern Europe, for example, alternative kinds of cavalry – with lighter equipment and peculiar tactical duties – had started to develop since the second half of the sixteenth century. As we have seen in the previous chapter, the new troop type of the lance-armed uhlans emerged in Poland. In Hungary, meanwhile, the light horsemen known as hussars gradually came to dominate the local battlefields.

The etymology of the word 'hussar' is not very clear, and over the years several theories have been elaborated in order to explain how this term came to indicate the light cavalrymen of Hungary. Most etymologists and historians, however, agree on the fact that the word could come from the Hungarian *'huszár'*, a modified version of the medieval Serbian *'husar'*, a word that was used to indicate the mounted brigands who harassed the peasant communities living in the countryside of the Balkan nations. In 1526, the expanding Ottoman Empire of the Turks defeated and invaded the Kingdom of Hungary, which together with Poland had been one of the leading political and military powers of eastern Europe during the Middle Ages. The Ottomans occupied most of the Hungarian lands, but not the region of Transylvania, which retained a degree of autonomy. During the second half of the sixteenth century, the territory of Hungary became the main battleground for the bloody wars that took place between the Habsburg Empire and the Ottoman Empire. These conflicts, which continued for most of the seventeenth century, were mostly fought for possession of Hungary, the Habsburgs being determined to eradicate the Turkish presence in the northern Balkans, which represented a serious threat to the political stability of their Austrian homeland. Initially, the Ottomans obtained a series of victories during these wars, but the Habsburgs eventually gained the upper hand. By the end of the seventeenth century, Transylvania had been annexed to the Austrian Empire, together with some other Hungarian territories. The Habsburgs had also started to exert their political control also over Croatia, which had been a vassal state of Hungary for most of the Middle Ages.

During the seventeenth century, the Balkans was almost constantly in a state of war, both the Habsburgs and the Turks employing bands of irregulars to conduct raids across their respective borders, even when there was no 'official' conflict going on. These irregulars, perceived as simple brigands by the local communities, acted in a very autonomous way and had no military discipline to speak of. They pillaged the frontier territories of their enemies and killed civilians with no mercy, earning a living as land-based pirates. These early hussars were not paid for their services but were of great use to the Habsburgs and the Ottomans, who could thus maintain a virtual state of war on the Balkan frontier without deploying their regular troops in that theatre of operations (which had significant economic costs). The harsh nature of the local terrain and the tactical duties that they had to perform made the hussars a very peculiar category of mounted troops: in order to move very rapidly on the hills and in the woods of the Balkans to conduct their guerrilla operations, they were mounted on agile but sturdy horses and carried light equipment consisting of offensive weapons only (they wore no helmets or armour to maintain a high degree of mobility).

Over time, the Habsburgs tried to regularize their bands of hussars recruited from Hungary and Croatia, understanding that these mounted skirmishers could be of great use in other theatres of operations outside the Balkans. In the early seventeenth century, the hussars started to add light firearms to their equipment and a good number of them – mostly those from Croatia – were employed in central Europe during the Thirty Years War. Both the Austrians and their opponents were greatly impressed by the combat abilities of the hussars, who were able to conduct effective reconnaissance missions as well as to harass enemy columns by using hit-and-run tactics. France, among Austria's main enemies during the Thirty Years War, was one of the first European nations to recruit irregular contingents of Croatian mercenaries for service in its armies. These, in 1667, were assembled together in order to form a regiment of Croatian light cavalry known as the Régiment Royal-Cravates Cavalerie. One piece of cloth worn by the Croatian soldiers in French service attracted the attention of other European leaders: the picturesque red scarf that they tied in a knot around their neck as part of their traditional dress. This served for protection against dust and sweat, but could also be used for dressing woods. The French soon adopted the scarf as part of their cavalry's dress, starting to wear neckties '*à la Croate*' that later became known as *cravates* (cravats). Soon after its regularization, the Royal Croatian Regiment lost its original status of being a light cavalry unit and was transformed into a corps of heavy cavalry, its original members gradually replaced by ordinary French troopers. During the late seventeenth century, the Habsburgs also started to recruit some regular units of hussars from their Hungarian territories, the semi-autonomous Principality of Transylvania having finally been annexed to Austrian control.

During the War of the Grand Alliance (1688–97), which saw the Kingdom of France fighting against a large military alliance that included Austria, the Habsburgs deployed three regiments of Hungarian hussars. These performed well and their military achievements were noticed by Louis XIV of France, who decided to organize some units of hussars inside his own armies. France, however, could not count on any community of frontier soldiers from which the new hussars could be recruited, so had no choice but to employ foreign mercenaries to create its own corps of hussars. The light horsemen of the Habsburgs came from the 'military frontier' of Croatia and Slavonia or from the border territories of Hungary, so they were experienced fighters who had spent most of their lives fighting against the Turks to defend their homeland. Finding mercenaries with such military expertise was not easy for Louis XIV, but by 1692 the first hussar regiment had been raised in the French Army. Known as the Hussards Royaux (Royal Hussars), they were recruited from Hungarian deserters of the Austrian Army. In 1698, however, the corps was disbanded following the end of the War of the Grand Alliance. Yet the French military authorities understood that the hussars had great military potential, since – unlike the heavy cavalry – they were capable of raiding sources of fodder and provisions during military campaigns, as well as pursuing fleeing enemy troops after a victory. As a result, during the years that followed the disbandment of the Hussards Royaux, several attempts were made to create a new unit of hussars in the French Army. The Hungarian light cavalry were used to fighting in open order and were famous for being excellent marksmen; training French horsemen to perform in this fashion was not an easy task, which was the main reason behind the early difficulties experienced by France while attempting to raise new regiments of hussars. In 1701, following the outbreak of the War of the Spanish Succession, the Royal Hussars Regiment was re-formed with Hungarian soldiers whose services were offered to France by Bavaria (an ally of Louis XIV). In 1719, Count Berchény, a Hungarian political exile living in France, was ordered to recruit a new regiment of hussars for the French Army from the lands of the

Ottoman Empire. Then in 1734, during the War of the Polish Succession, Count Estherazy (another Hungarian political exile living in France) raised a third regiment of hussars in Strasbourg from deserters of the Austrian Army. During the War of the Austrian Succession (1740–48), another four regiments of French hussars were created, bringing the total to seven.

Following the outbreak of the Seven Years' War, the French government decided in 1762 to consolidate the existing units of hussars into just three regiments. These gradually lost their original foreign character, their members starting to be ordinary French horsemen who received the same training as the original Hungarian hussars. With the end of the wars fought against the Austrian Empire, France no longer had access to significant numbers of Hungarian deserters from whom its hussars could be recruited. Several of the hussar regiments' officers, however, were still Hungarian aristocrats who had rebelled against the Habsburgs during recent years and had later established themselves in France as political exiles. In 1764, a fourth regiment of hussars was created, then in 1779, three of the existing regiments were required to provide one squadron each for the formation of a fifth hussar regiment. In addition, all the hussar corps of the French Army were put under the overall command of a superior officer known as the Colonel-General of the Hussars. In May 1780, to support the war efforts of the Thirteen Colonies that were fighting for their independence from Great Britain, France sent a large expeditionary corps to North America. This comprised a unit known as Lauzun's Legion that was mostly recruited from German, Polish and Irish mercenaries who were in search of employment in the French military. Command of the corps was given to Armand Louis de Gontaut, Duke of Lauzun, who had already served in the French Army and was an experienced officer with an adventurous temperament. During the second half of the eighteenth century, the French Army created several units known as legions, miniature armies comprising sub-units of infantry, cavalry and artillery. The basic idea behind their formation was to have some corps that could act independently from the rest of the army as they comprised soldiers from every branch of service. Lauzun's Legion consisted of one company of grenadiers, one company of chasseurs, two companies of fusiliers, one company of artillery and two companies of hussars (each of the latter consisting of one troop equipped with lances and one equipped only with sabres). Once in North America, the corps fought with great determination and distinguished itself during a cavalry clash that took place at Gloucester (not far from Yorktown), where the hussars commanded by Lauzun defeated the famous light dragoons of Banastre Tarleton's British Legion. In June 1783, the French expeditionary corps left North America and returned home, but while the foot components of Lauzun's

Legion were all disbanded, the mounted units were transformed into a new regiment of hussars of the French Army.

Consequently, by the outbreak of the French Revolution, the nation's military forces comprised a total of six hussar units. In 1791, following the reforms of the new republican government, the hussars lost their traditional aristocratic denominations and were given distinctive progressive numbers: the Berchény Regiment became the 1st Hussars, the Chamborant Regiment was named the 2nd Hussars, the Conflans Regiment became the 3rd Hussars, the Estherazy Regiment was renamed the 4th Hussars, the Colonel-General Regiment's new denomination was the 5th Hussars and the Lauzun Regiment became the 6th Hussars. In 1792, the former Conflans Regiment mutinied and joined the ranks of the anti-republican military forces that were organizing a counter-revolution; as a result, the number of hussar corps was briefly reduced to five and the unit number of the former Conflans Regiment was given to the former Estherazy Regiment. The Colonel-General Regiment then became the 4th Hussars and the Lauzun Regiment the 5th Hussars. According to the new internal structure introduced in 1786, each hussar unit consisted of four squadrons with two companies each. During the turbulent years of the Revolutionary Wars, several new units of volunteer hussars were formed, these corps usually being made up of young volunteers who wanted to emulate the traditional dash and uniforms of the 'real' hussars. These units were, however, quite short-lived and could be organized in many different ways. Some of them were quite large, while others consisted of just a few 'well-to-do' gentlemen from the middle classes of Paris. The new units of volunteer hussars wore colourful uniforms and bore resonant denominations such as the Freedom Hussars or Death's Head Hussars, but had little military capability compared with the regular hussars. As a result, following the end of the military crisis that culminated with the Battle of Valmy in 1792, the French authorities decided to disband the various corps of volunteer hussars and to employ their best elements to create some new regular regiments.

The 6th and 7th Hussars were formed on 23 November 1792, soon followed by further new regiments numbered 8–11 during 1793. The 12th Hussars was created in 1794 and the 13th Hussars in 1795. The latter was a very short-lived corps, being disbanded the following year. In addition to these units there was a 7th Hussars 'bis', a former volunteer corps that was transformed into a regular formation. As a result of this expansion, when Napoleon became First Consul of the Republic in 1799, the French Army comprised a total of 13 hussar regiments (including the 'bis' corps). During the following years, Napoleon raised no new units of hussars, preferring to augment his light cavalry by organizing new corps of mounted chasseurs. In 1803, three of the existing regiments of hussars were converted into dragoon units: the

Officer of the 4th Regiment of Hussars.

11th Hussars became the 29th Regiment of Dragoons, the 12th Hussars became the 30th Dragoons and the 7th Hussars 'bis' was transformed into the 28th Dragoons. In that same year, a new internal structure was introduced for the regiments of hussars, with each unit to consist of four squadrons with two companies each, the 1st Company of the 1st Squadron known as the Elite Company. The regimental staff of a hussar corps was to comprise the following elements: one regiment commander, three squadron commanders, two adjutant-majors, one quartermaster-paymaster, one surgeon-major, two adjutant-NCOs, one veterinary officer, one trumpet-major, one

Officer of the 6th Regiment of Hussars.

blacksmith, one craftsman-saddler, one craftsman-tailor, one craftsman-cobbler and one craftsman-armourer. Each company comprised of one captain, one lieutenant, two second lieutenants, one chief staff sergeant, four staff sergeants, one brigadier-fourrier, four brigadiers, two trumpeters and eighty troopers. In 1806, the composition of the regimental staff was slightly changed to include the following: one colonel, one major, three squadron commanders, two adjutant-majors, one quartermaster-paymaster, one surgeon-major, one aide-surgeon, two surgeons, two adjutant-NCOs, one veterinary officer, one trumpet-brigadier, one craftsman-saddler, one craftsman-tailor, one craftsman-cobbler and one craftsman-armourer. At the same time, each company adopted the following structure: one captain, one lieutenant, two second lieutenants, one chief staff sergeant, four staff sergeants, one brigadier-fourrier, eight brigadiers, two trumpeters and eighty-four troopers. On 9 March 1809, a ninth company – acting as depot formation – was added to each hussar regiment.

In 1810, following the annexation of the Kingdom of Holland to the French Empire, the former 2nd Hussar Regiment of the Dutch Army became the new 11th Hussar

Troopers of the 1st Regiment of Hussars.

Troopers of the 5th Regiment of Hussars.

Regiment of the French Army. In 1812, the number of squadrons in each regiment was increased to six and the depot company was disbanded. The composition of the regimental staff then became as follows: one colonel, one major, two squadron commanders, one quartermaster-paymaster, one surgeon-major, one aide-surgeon, two surgeons, one orderly, two adjutant-NCOs, two veterinary officers, one trumpet-brigadier, one craftsman-saddler, one craftsman-tailor, one craftsman-cobbler and one craftsman-armourer. Meanwhile, companies had the following structure: one captain, one lieutenant, two second lieutenants, one chief staff sergeant, four staff sergeants, one brigadier-fourrier, eight brigadiers, two trumpeters, one blacksmith and 108 troopers. In January 1812 three squadrons of the 9th Hussars that were serving in Spain were temporarily detached from their parent unit in order to form a new 9th Hussars 'bis', which itself was transformed into the new 12th Hussar Regiment in 1813. The last expansion of the French hussars came in 1813, following the disastrous invasion of Russia, when Napoleon decided to use the conscripts from the Italian departments of his empire to create two new units of hussars. The 13th Regiment of Hussars was organized with recruits from the departments of central Italy, while the 14th Hussars comprised recruits from northern Italy. The 13th Hussars was dissolved on 13 December 1813 after having suffered severe losses, but was re-raised in January 1814 by using the former members of a foreign hussar unit that had recently been disbanded (the 'Jérôme-Napoléon' Regiment of the Westphalian Army). The 14th Hussars was disbanded on 11 November 1813, but it too was soon reorganized after absorbing the former members of other recently dissolved cavalry units. With the first restoration of the Bourbons in 1814, only the first six regiments of hussars were retained in service. Consequently, Napoleon fought his Belgian campaign with an insufficient number of light cavalry units in 1815.

Napoleon used his light cavalry in a very effective and innovative manner during his campaigns between 1805 and 1815. His hussars conducted long-range reconnaissance missions but were also employed – quite frequently – for rear and outpost protection of the main marching columns. The emperor's light cavalry were also used to perform defensive duties in addition to their usual offensive ones. During the Prussian campaign of 1806, for example, Napoleon formed an independent Light Cavalry Brigade consisting of the 5th and 7th Hussars, which excelled under the orders of General Lasalle. The archetype of the hussar, Lasalle had an anarchic character and was a daring adventurer. Famed for his personal exploits, which included love affairs and many duels, Lasalle was a perfect light cavalry commander, with great personal skills. During the campaign of 1806, his hussar brigade soon became known as the 'Brigade Infernale' (Hellish Brigade), moving rapidly on enemy territory in order to gather information as well as food supplies. After the French victory at the Battle of Jena, Lasalle moved towards the Prussian city of Stettin and arrived well ahead of the main French force. Stettin was well fortified and defended by a large garrison of over 5,000 Prussian soldiers, who could count on 160 artillery guns of different calibre. Lasalle, giving the impression that the entire French Army had arrived, demanded the surrender of the city. The Prussian defenders did not realize that the French officer and his few hussars were instigating a gigantic bluff and thus, fearing that there was no hope of escape, decided to surrender without a fight. When Napoleon was informed that just two regiments of hussars (500 men in total) had captured

Stettin, he wrote the following message to his cavalry commander, Murat: 'If your Light Cavalry captures fortified towns, I'll have to discharge my Engineer Corps and have my heavy artillery melted down.'

Despite being confined for the most part to scouring the countryside in the vicinity of the main columns of French troops, the hussar regiments proved they were also able to charge against enemy infantry if needed. Furthermore, when engaged on the open field by a superior enemy mounted force, the hussars were trained to form a

Troopers of the 8th Regiment of Hussars.

Musician of the 3rd Regiment of Hussars.

screen of sharpshooters along their front and to slow down the movements of their opponents by firing at enemy officers. Napoleon's light cavalrymen were also capable of maintaining surveillance of their opponents by forcing a contact and of masking the true movements of their army's main columns by using feints. The *esprit de corps* of the hussar regiments was unparalleled in the French cavalry, based on a mixture of audacity and arrogance. Sometimes criticized by the more traditionalist officers because of their slack discipline, the hussars were praised by their emperor because of their tactical creativity and incredible audacity.

Uniforms and equipment

The 'excesses' of the French hussars were particularly evident in their colourful uniforms, which were based – like those worn by all the hussar units of the European armies – on the traditional dress of the original Hungarian hussars. The egotism of the French light cavalrymen was clearly visible in their near-anarchic mode of dress, which was admired across Europe. The hussars' uniform consisted of two main elements: a short shell-jacket known as a dolman and a jacket slung on the left shoulder known as a pelisse. These were both adorned with several rows of buttons and frogging, and were worn together with tight riding breeches decorated with colourful embroidering and with calf-length boots. The personal equipment of the hussars was also distinctive, including a curved sabre with sword-knot, a black leather cartridge pouch, a barrel sash worn around the waist, short gloves and a sabretache. The latter was a flat pouch attached to the belt of the sabre that was used to transport documents; it was strongly associated with the hussars and was decorated with rich embroidering. Differently from the other cavalry units of the French Army that had uniforms in distinctive colours (blue for the cuirassiers and green for the dragoons, for example), the hussar regiments were distinguished from one another by the different colours of their dolmans, pelisses and breeches, as well as of their uniforms' facings. As a result of this, the dress worn by the French hussars during the Napoleonic Wars presented a bewildering variety.

Until 1803, the headgear of the hussars was a shako of the mirliton type, which was characterized by the presence of a *'flamme'* or turban that was wrapped around its body and of a detachable peak on its front. This early shako was 19cm tall and 22cm in diameter; it had a coloured plume and a tricolour cockade on the left side. The *flamme* of the mirliton was in the facing colour of each regiment, while the main body of the shako was black. Coloured cords and flounders were frequently wrapped around the headgear and the turban. In 1803, a new model of shako was introduced after the following modifications were made to the previous one: both the *flamme* and the detachable peak were removed, the cockade and plume were moved to the front of the headgear and a plate was added beneath the cockade. The brass plate was lozenge-shaped and bore the regimental number. The shako was held in place by a strap that passed beneath the wearer's plaited hair queue, and a cord was attached to the uniform in order to prevent the loss of the headgear should it be toppled. During 1805/06, the shako was slightly modified in its shape, becoming taller and more bell-shaped, with its strap replaced by brass chinscales. As a result of these changes, a new model of shako came into use in 1806. Decorative cords and flounders, although redundant, continued to be worn with this new version of the headgear. The Elite Company of each regiment, rather than shakos, wore black bearskin colpacks similar to busbies. These could have decorative cords and flounders like the shakos. Each colpack had a 'bag' of cloth in the same colour as the pelisse on one of its two sides (piped and tasselled in the same colour as the dolman's frogging) and a coloured plume on the front. The trumpeters of Elite Companies had white colpacks instead of the usual black ones. The use of the bearskin colpack became increasingly popular, and this kind of elite headgear also started to be worn by the officers and trumpeters of the standard companies. According to the official dress regulations, however, the trumpeters of the standard companies were to use shakos in the colour of their dolman.

On 9 November 1810, the use of decorative cords and flounders was officially abolished and the coloured tall plumes (which were black for most of the regiments and red for the Elite Companies) worn on the front of the headgear were replaced by a simple lentil-shaped pompom made of wool. These modifications, however, never became particularly popular and were applied only very slowly. The new dress regulations of 1812 prohibited the use of colpacks for the Elite Companies, prescribing instead a peculiar shako that was 10mm taller and wider than that worn by ordinary troopers. This elite headgear had a top band, bottom band and side chevrons in red as marks of distinction. The new shako also had a different version of the frontal plate, consisting of a crescent (bearing unit number) surmounted by an imperial eagle. This too was never popular and was adopted by just a few Elite Companies, most of which preferred to retain their usual colpacks. In 1812, a new model of informal shako was introduced for the centre companies, which was known as the *shako rouleau* because of its shape. This was taller than its predecessor – exceeding 20cm in height – and consisted of a reinforced black felt cylinder that was often covered with coloured fabric. It had a black leather peak on the front and a fold-down neck cover at the rear, and had no brass plate on the front. The *shako rouleau* never became regulation issue, but by 1814 it had replaced the previous model of bell-shaped shako in most of the regiments. For trumpeters, the new headgear was covered with fabric in the same colour as the pelisse. Off-duty, all hussars wore the standard *bonnet de police* fatigue cap in regimental colours, replaced after 1812 by the new *pokalem* headgear. Officers used their own versions of the different headgear described above, having silver or golden top bands for the shakos and silver or golden cords and flounders for the colpacks. Off-duty, they frequently wore black bicorn hats instead of the usual fatigue caps.

The dolman was fastened along its entire length by eighteen semi-circular buttons and their corresponding braid loops, while the pelisse's loops were cut so that only the top five were long enough to be used. Both garments had five rows of buttons

The Hussars

Trumpeter of the 7th Regiment of Hussars.

on the front, but there were some regiments with only three rows. The pelisse was secured on the shoulder by a length of doubled-over cord that passed over the right shoulder and was then looped about a toggle sewn to the opposite side of the collar. The dolman had a standing collar and pointed cuffs piped in a contrasting colour, while the pelisse was bordered with black fur. The frontal frogging of the dolman and the pelisse was in the same colour as the collar/cuffs' piping, while the pelisse also had piping in this colour on its pointed cuffs. The breeches were in the same colour as the dolman, having side-stripes and decorative embroidering on the front – known as 'Hungarian knots' – in the same colour as the jackets' frontal frogging. As a result of the above, each regiment had at least three different distinctive colours, which were used to produce the various garments according to the following scheme:

Regiment	Dolman	Collar	Cuffs	Pelisse	Breeches	Frogging
1st Hussars	Sky blue	Sky blue	Red	Sky blue	Sky blue	White
2nd Hussars	Brown	Brown	Sky blue	Brown	Sky blue	White
3rd Hussars	Grey	Grey	Red	Grey	Grey	White
4th Hussars	Dark blue	Dark blue	Red	Red	Dark blue	Yellow
5th Hussars	Sky blue	Sky blue	White	White	Sky blue	Yellow
6th Hussars	Red	Red	Red	Dark blue	Dark blue	Yellow
7th Hussars	Dark green	Red	Red	Dark green	Red	Yellow
8th Hussars	Dark green	Red	Red	Dark green	Red	White
9th Hussars	Red	Sky blue	Sky blue	Sky blue	Sky blue	Yellow
10th Hussars	Sky blue	Red	Red	Sky blue	Sky blue	White
11th Hussars	Dark blue	Red	Red	Dark blue	Dark blue	Yellow
12th Hussars	Red	Sky blue	Red	Sky blue	Sky blue	White
13th Hussars	Brown	Sky blue	Sky blue	Brown	Sky blue	White
14th Hussars	Dark green	Red	Red	Dark green	Red	White

When the frogging was white for troopers, it was silver for officers; when it was yellow for troopers, it was golden for officers. Rank was shown by inverted chevrons applied above the pointed cuffs of the dolman and pelisse, in white or yellow for troopers and NCOs and silver or golden for officers. Years of service for troopers/NCOs were shown by inverted white or yellow chevrons applied on the left sleeve of the dolman and pelisse. The Hungarian knots embroidered on the front of the breeches also indicated rank, those of officers consisting of more stripes of lace, their number corresponding to a specific rank. These decorative knots were in the same colour as the frogging and had different shapes according to each regiment, but most of them were simple trefoils or bastion-shaped loops. After 1806, as an alternative to the dolman and pelisse, the hussars were given a simple single-breasted coat known as a *kinski*, which had a standing collar, pointed cuffs and short tails. Designed for campaign use, it was very practical to wear. The *kinski* was in the colour of the dolman, had collar and cuffs like those of the dolman and was piped (on the front and on the tails) in the same colour as the pelisse. The dress regulations of 1812 prescribed that a slim braid shoulder-strap be sewn to the left shoulder of the dolman and pelisse to secure the webbing.

As an alternative to the tight Hungarian breeches, on campaign the hussars could wear much more comfortable overalls, which were in the same colour as the breeches but opened down the side by means of eighteen bone or pewter buttons along the

Trumpeter of the 10th Regiment of Hussars.

outer seams. The inside leg and cuffs of these overalls were reinforced with black leather. The dress regulations of 1812 simplified the Hungarian knots of the breeches, ordering that they had to be bastion-shaped for all regiments, and also officially recognized the use of the overalls for campaign service. By 1812, the overalls had already been modified, given a front fly concealed by a flap and now bearing coloured lace or piping on the length of the outer seams. The boots used by the hussars were of the classic Hungarian variety, with the top edge bordered with piping and a frontal tassel in white or yellow (silver or golden for officers). Belt equipment was white and all ranks wore wrist-length white gloves when riding.

Trumpeters were dressed like the ordinary hussars, but with the colpack as headgear and with all the garments having reversed colours. The colpack and the pelisse's edging were often made of white fur for musicians. The new Imperial Livery introduced for all musicians in 1812 never became popular in the hussar regiments. Curiously, some units of hussars included a squad of sappers within their regimental staff; these elite soldiers wore the colpack instead of the shako and had a specific red badge (consisting of two crossed axes under a flaming grenade) embroidered on the sleeves of their dolman and pelisse.

The sword-knot of all hussars was black leather until 1801, later becoming white buff. The *sabretache* flat pouch had a frontal flap bearing the regimental number encircled by a wreath of laurel leaves, but there were several alternative devices that usually also included an imperial eagle. The flap of the *sabretache* was covered in cloth in a diversity of colours and was decorated with elaborately embroidered motifs; as a result, it was so valuable that a leather cover was generally slipped over it on the march or in action. A small brass shield with regimental number and imperial eagle was usually applied on the front of these protective covers. The 1812 regulations prescribed a general rationalization of the *sabretache*'s decorations, but were rarely respected by the various regiments. The barrel-sash worn by all ranks around the waist had alternating vertical bands in two colours: white/yellow (according to the colour of the frogging) and the colour of the pelisse.

The saddle-cloth consisted of a white or black half-shabraque made of sheepskin that was edged with small triangles of cloth in the same colour as the breeches, and a shabraque in the same colour as the breeches – edged in white/yellow for rankers/NCOs or in silver/golden for officers – that had a white/yellow or silver/golden regimental number on the back corner. Most of the superior officers had privately purchased exotic shabraques made from the skin of a leopard or tiger. The external edge of the officers' shabraques consisted of a different number of stripes of lace that corresponded to a specific rank.

The main weapon of the hussars was the 'Year IV' model light cavalry sabre, which had a curved blade and hilt/scabbard fittings made of iron. Around 1807, this started to be replaced with the new sabres of the 'Year IX' and 'Year XI' models, which had an N-shaped copper basket guard and iron scabbard. Troopers also carried a flintlock musketoon, which could be of the 1786 model or of the later 'Year IX' model. Trumpeters, NCOs and officers did not have the musketoon, but instead carried a couple of flintlock pistols, which could be of the old 1763 model or the newer 'Year XIII' model.

Chapter 6

The Mounted Chasseurs

History and organization

At the beginning of the eighteenth century, line infantry tactics and formations were extremely static: while moving on the battlefield, the line infantrymen advanced in columns, but they deployed into long lines when stopping to open fire upon the enemy. After several rolling volleys of musketry were exchanged between two opposing infantry formations, a clash could continue in two different ways. On most occasions, one of the two lines was shattered by the enemy fire and thus decided to retreat, but on others it was necessary to fight hand-to-hand with the bayonet to determine the outcome of the confrontation. Keeping order in the formations and delivering a regular fire were the key factors behind victory, meaning training was absolutely vital to transform the line infantry corps into an effective tactical tool. Generally speaking, battles were extremely static, maintaining perfect order in their formations obliging both the infantrymen and the heavy cavalry to move very slowly. The transition from column formation to line was extremely delicate, since it exposed the fusiliers to sudden charges by enemy cavalry. When confronting horsemen, line infantry usually adopted a defensive formation known as the square, another kind of close order that had been in practice for many years, with the intention of stopping enemy attacks by using the bayonets as 'pikes' against mounted troops. The success of these infantry formations and tactics was determined by the performance of the muskets that were in use during the eighteenth century. These were flintlock weapons, for which the loading operation was quite complicated. The muskets of this period were all smoothbores and thus were extremely inaccurate as when a projectile was fired, it came out from the weapon without a precise direction since there were no grooves inside the barrel to guide it to its target. In consequence, during a battle, line infantry formations had to come very close together in order to use their weapons effectively. The muskets of the age were also extremely heavy, which greatly limited the mobility of the foot soldiers. When moving over broken terrain, for example, it was practically impossible for them to keep close formations in order. All the main tactical formations were thus created for an ideal battlefield, consisting of a large plain where the opposing infantry and cavalry could move without encountering obstacles.

Due to the various technical limitations described above, the heavy cavalry units made a very limited use of firearms. A couple of flintlock pistols were generally carried by each horseman, but these could be fired only from short distances and thus were of little use. Dragoons, as we have seen, also carried flintlock muskets or musketoons, but these were generally used only when they dismounted to fight on foot. In the military system of the early eighteenth century, soldiers were not required to think or to act in an autonomous way: they only had to move like clockwork in order to put in practice the orders they received. There was no space for initiative, any infraction of discipline immediately punished with very harsh methods. The movements required on the battlefield were repeated every day during training sessions, under the incessant beat of the drums. A classic example of this kind of eighteenth-century warfare was the Prussian Army of Frederick the Great, who perfected close line infantry and heavy cavalry tactics and was admired by all the officer corps of Europe. During the War of the Austrian Succession (1740–48) and the Seven Years' War (1756–63), however, several episodes showed that the Prussian heavy infantry and heavy cavalry were not as perfect as they may seem. It became apparent that units operating in close order could experience serious problems while operating on broken terrain and when fighting against an enemy that employed hit-and-run tactics. In particular, the Prussians had serious problems in countering the efficient light troops deployed by the Austrian Empire, which also included hussars. Each of these light troops was capable of advancing in open order on the battlefield while keeping contact with other members of his unit, so he could cover his advance behind obstacles on the terrain (like a tree, for example) and fire upon the enemy from a favourable position. As a result, during the War of the Austrian Succession and Seven Years' War, the Hungarian light cavalrymen of the Austrian Army caused serious trouble and losses to Frederick the Great's heavy mounted troops.

After the end of the War of the Austrian Succession, most of the major European armies saw a general expansion of their light cavalry units, a situation that continued for several decades, combat experience in the Seven Years' War doing nothing but confirm the tactical importance of the new light corps. A new form of warfare was thus born: the *petite guerre* (little war), which was based on low-intensity combat and hit-and-run tactics. France was one of the first European countries to understand the importance of the new light corps, recruiting several units of light infantry and light cavalry during the Seven Years' War. These, however, were all of only a temporary nature, most of them being disbanded when hostilities came to an end in 1763. Some years later, in 1776, the French government finally decided to create a permanent corps of light troops within its cavalry (in addition to the hussars). As a result, the existing independent units of light horsemen that had not been disbanded after 1763 were assembled together to form twenty-four squadrons of mounted chasseurs. These new squadrons of light cavalry were not designed to act as independent corps, each of them being attached to a regiment of dragoons. At that time, mounted chasseurs were still considered an auxiliary component of the line cavalry, and thus were organized in small units. However, the mounted chasseurs soon showed their great combat capability and tactical flexibility. Consequently, in 1779, the twenty-four squadrons raised three years beforehand were detached from the units of dragoons and instead assembled together to form six independent regiments of mounted chasseurs, having four squadrons each.

In 1784, the French decided to create permanent and regular units of light infantry for their army, following the lessons learned during the American Revolution. Six battalions of foot chasseurs were organized, each of them attached to one of the existing regiments of mounted chasseurs in order to form new light corps of an experimental nature (each of them comprising four companies of foot chasseurs and four squadrons of mounted chasseurs). In 1788, having seen that the composite nature of the chasseur regiments was quite limiting for both the infantry companies and the cavalry squadrons, it was decided to separate the foot chasseurs from the mounted chasseurs. The mounted chasseurs were reorganized on twelve regiments, numbered 1–12. The first six regiments were created by converting six existing dragoon corps into units of mounted chasseurs, while the remaining ones were formed by using the squadrons of mounted chasseurs that were already in existence. Each of the new units was given a particular denomination, deriving from the area of France from which it was raised. With the reorganization of the mounted chasseurs on twelve regiments, the French Army had the largest number of regular light cavalry corps of any European nation. In many ways, the mounted chasseurs were the French equivalent of the Hungarian hussars, performing the same tactical duties and being given light personal equipment.

During the Revolutionary Wars, the number of French mounted chasseur regiments was greatly expanded, with thirteen new units of this kind established during the period 1793–95. Following the military crisis of 1792, thousands of young volunteers decided to serve under the flag of the new French Republic in order to defend their homeland from the armies of various invading foreign powers. Many new units of volunteer cavalry were thus created across France and sent to the front to join the regular forces. The new volunteer corps of cavalry mostly had light equipment and comprised young patriots who were full of enthusiasm but had no combat experience, meaning their military performance varied widely. Some units were well uniformed and large in number, whereas others were too small and undisciplined to exist for more than a few months. From 1793, the new French government tried to rationalize

Mounted chasseur with dolman.

the many units of volunteer light cavalry by gathering them together to form several new regular corps of mounted chasseurs. In 1793, new mounted chasseur regiments numbered 13–24 were created using this method, followed by the 25th Mounted Chasseurs during 1794. In 1795, however, two of the new units (the 17th and 18th Mounted Chasseurs) were disbanded when their members – who were all Belgian volunteers – returned to their homeland. The numbers of these two regiments remained vacant until the end of the Napoleonic Wars.

As a result of the above organizational changes, by the beginning of his rule as First Consul of France, Napoleon could count on a total of twenty-three mounted chasseur regiments. In 1802, that number rose to twenty-four with the creation of the new 26th Mounted Chasseurs, which was formed by recruiting former members of the Piedmontese Legion's cavalry. In 1799, what remained of the Piedmontese Army had been absorbed into the French Army, Piedmont (officially known as the Kingdom of Sardinia) having been annexed to France. The Piedmontese soldiers were reorganized on two demi-brigades of line infantry, one demi-brigade of light infantry, one regiment of dragoons and one regiment of mounted chasseurs, but these units were quite short-lived and were all disbanded in 1802. The former Piedmontese cavalrymen were therefore employed to raise the new 26th Mounted Chasseurs.

The Mounted Chasseurs

Mounted chasseur with dolman.

Each regiment of mounted chasseurs consisted of four squadrons, each of which comprised two companies. The 1st Company of the 1st Squadron, like with the hussars, was known as the Elite Company. In addition to the four active squadrons, each regiment also comprised two non-combatant depot squadrons. The staff of each mounted chasseur regiment consisted of the following elements: one colonel, one major, two lieutenant-colonels, one quartermaster, one surgeon-major, one chaplain, two adjutants, one trumpet-major and five master-artisans. A single company comprised the following: one captain, one lieutenant, one second lieutenant, one senior staff sergeant, four junior staff sergeants, one fourrier, eight brigadiers, one trumpeter and eighty-two troopers. Each company consisted of two troops and thus had a very flexible structure. In 1807, the composition of the regimental staff was changed as follows: one colonel, one major, two squadron commanders, two adjutant-majors, one paymaster-quartermaster, one surgeon-major, one assistant-major, two sub-assistant majors, two adjutants, one trumpet-major, one veterinary surgeon and six artisans (the latter being cobblers, tailors, armourers and saddlers).

Between 1808 and 1811, Napoleon expanded his mounted chasseurs by raising five new regiments, numbered 27–31. Each of these had their own distinctive history and

Mounted chasseurs with *habit-long*. The farrier on the left and the officer of an elite company on the right are wearing the busby instead of the standard shako.

Officer of the mounted chasseurs with M1812 dress.

most of them were made up of non-French soldiers. The 27th Mounted Chasseurs was organized in September 1806 by the Duke Prosper-Louis d'Arenberg, who raised it from the Belgian territories and equipped it at his own expense. Belgium was at that time already part of the French Empire, but the cavalry corps established by the Duke d'Arenberg remained an autonomous unit in the early years that followed its creation. The unit bore the official denomination of Chevau-Légers Belges du Duc d'Arenberg (Belgian Light Cavalrymen of the Duke d'Arenberg). After reviewing

Troopers of the mounted chasseurs with M1812 uniform.

The Mounted Chasseurs

Trooper of the mounted chasseurs with M1812 dress.

the regiment, Napoleon was greatly impressed by its discipline and decided to absorb it into the mounted chasseurs of the French Army; on 29 May 1808, the Belgian Light Cavalrymen of the Duke d'Arenberg became the new 27th Mounted Chasseurs. Since 1801 the Grand Duchy of Tuscany, one of many Italian states, had been transformed by the French into a puppet realm known as the Kingdom of Etruria, which had a small army that comprised a single good-quality dragoon regiment. In December 1807, Napoleon absorbed the Kingdom of Etruria into his empire and thus the small Tuscan military forces became part of the French Army, the Etrurian dragoons becoming the 28th Mounted Chasseurs in early 1808. During the same year, by assembling together several detachments from the regiments of mounted chasseurs that had been deployed in Spain, three new Régiments Provisories de Cavalerie Légère (Provisional Regiments of Light Cavalry) were formed. One of these, the 3rd Regiment, was transformed into a permanent corps as the 29th Mounted Chasseurs in 1810. The remaining two Régiments Provisories de Cavalerie Légère were joined together and turned into a permanent corps as the 31st Mounted Chasseurs in 1811. The 30th Mounted Chasseurs was formed in February 1811 from the German cavalrymen of the Hanoverian Legion (see chapter 12) and a dragoon regiment raised by the independent city of Hamburg. As we have already seen in Chapter 4, this unit was soon transformed into a lancer corps.

With the first restoration of the Bourbons in 1814, only fifteen regiments of mounted chasseurs were retained in French service, meaning that when Napoleon returned in 1815, he fought his Belgian campaign with under-strength light cavalry forces. During the Napoleonic Wars, the mounted chasseurs had fought with great valour, including during major pitched battles such as Austerlitz. They were famed for their great flexibility and were capable – if needed – of fighting on foot. From a tactical point of view, they performed exactly the same duties as the hussars, which have been described in the previous chapter. A strong rivalry existed between the mounted chasseurs and the hussars. The chasseurs thought they were the equals of the hussars, but the hussars believed otherwise. Such was their rivalry that frequent quarrels arose between the two, often on the most futile pretext.

Uniforms and equipment

Prior to 1803, the headgear of the mounted chasseurs was a shako of the mirliton type, which was characterized by a *flamme* or turban that was wrapped around its body and by a detachable peak that was applied to its front. This early shako, which was 19cm tall and 22cm wide, had a coloured plume (dark green with point in regimental colour) and a tricolour cockade on the left side. The *flamme* of the mirliton was in the distinctive colour of each regiment, while the main body of the shako was black. Coloured cords and flounders were frequently wrapped around the headgear, together with the turban. In 1803, a new model of shako was introduced with the following modifications: both the *flamme* and the detachable peak were removed, the cockade and the plume were moved to the front of the headgear and a plate was added beneath the cockade. The brass plate was lozenge-shaped and bore the regimental number. The shako was held in place by a strap that passed under the wearer's plaited queue. In 1805/06, the headgear was slightly modified in its shape, becoming taller and more bell-like, while its strap was replaced by brass chinscales. As a result of these changes, a new model of shako came into use in 1806. Decorative cords and flounders, although redundant, continued to be worn with this new version of the headgear. The Elite Company of each regiment, instead of havinge shakos, wore black bearskin busbie-like colpacks. These could have decorative cords and flounders like the shakos. Each colpack had a cloth 'bag' in the regimental colour on its left side that was piped and tasselled in white for NCOs/troopers and in silver for officers. The colpack had the usual coloured plume on the front, which was entirely red. The trumpeters of Elite Companies had white colpacks instead of the usual black ones. Over time, the use of the bearskin colpack became increasingly popular, this kind of elite headgear also starting to be worn by officers and the trumpeters of the standard companies. According to the official dress regulations, however, the trumpeters of the standard companies were to have shakos in regimental colours.

On 9 November 1810, the use of decorative cords and flounders was officially abolished and the coloured tall plumes (which were dark green with the point in regimental colour or entirely red for the Elite Companies) worn on the front of the headgear were replaced by a simple lentil-shaped pompom made of wool (in regimental colour or red for the Elite Companies). These modifications, however, never became particularly popular, and thus were applied only slowly. The new dress regulations of 1812 prohibited the use of colpacks for the Elite Companies and prescribed instead the wearing of a peculiar shako that was 10mm taller and wider than that worn by ordinary troopers. This elite headgear had top band, bottom band and side chevrons in red as marks of distinction. The new shako also had a different version of the front plate, consisting of a crescent (bearing unit number) surmounted by an imperial eagle. This shako was never popular and was adopted by just a few Elite Companies, since most of them preferred to retain their traditional colpacks. Off-duty, all mounted chasseurs wore the standard *bonnet de police* fatigue cap in dark green with piping and frontal tassel in regimental colour, which was replaced in 1812 by the new *pokalem* headgear. Both the *bonnet de police* and the *pokalem* had the distinctive badge of the mounted chasseurs (a bugle horn) embroidered in regimental colour on the front. Officers used their own versions of the different headgear described above, having silver top bands for the shakos and silver cords and flounders for the colpacks. Off-duty, they frequently wore black bicorn hats instead of the usual fatigue caps.

From their foundation, the mounted chasseurs were dressed in dark green, with facings in distinctive regimental colours. During the Revolutionary Wars and up to 1806, they wore a uniform in clear hussar-style that comprised a dolman but not a pelisse. The dolman of the mounted chasseurs was dark green, with standing collar and pointed cuffs in regimental colour. It was fastened along its entire length by between thirteen and eighteen semi-circular pewter buttons and white braid loops. The jacket had three rows of buttons on the front and its collar and cuffs were piped in white, as were the waist, back-seams and front vent of the dolman. Some regiments also had dark green shoulder straps piped in white. The jackets of the officers were identical to those of the NCOs and rankers, but had five rows of buttons instead of three and their frogging/piping was silver rather than white. Rank was shown by white inverted chevrons applied above the pointed cuffs of the dolman, these chevrons being silver for officers. Years of service for troopers/NCOs were shown by white inverted chevrons applied on the left sleeve. Trumpeters had dolmans in regimental colour with facings in dark green.

Around 1806, the dolman was replaced by the *habit-long*, which had been worn until then as campaign dress. This consisted of a long-tailed and lapelled tunic that had the same colouring as the dolman jacket except for the following particulars: the dark green tails of the skirt were turned back to reveal the regimental colour and their turnbacks were adorned with a dark green bugle horn device; the standing collar and the pointed cuffs had piping in dark green rather than in white; the frontal lapels were dark green with piping in regimental colour; the new tunic had dark green shoulder straps piped in regimental colour; and on the back of the tails there were false vertical pockets with three buttons each that were piped in regimental colour. The officers' rank was now shown by silver epaulettes worn on the shoulders. Under the *habit-long*, the mounted chasseurs wore a sleeveless single-breasted waistcoat that was dark green in the winter and white in the summer. Quite frequently, however, this item of dress was in regimental colour and was double-breasted instead of single-breasted. In addition, it was quite common for waistcoats to have coloured frontal frogging like the old dolmans. Trumpeters wore the *habit-long* with reversed colours and had white epaulettes, while the mounted chasseurs of the Elite Companies had red epaulettes.

The simple single-breasted coat known as the *kinski* came into use in 1808. This was dark green and had standing collar, pointed cuffs and short tails. Being designed for campaign use, it was very practical to wear. The *kinski* had collar and cuffs like those

The Mounted Chasseurs

Trumpeters of the mounted chasseurs wearing their pre-1812 uniforms in bright colours.

Musicians of the mounted chasseurs with pre-1812 regimental dress.

of the *habit-long* and was piped (on the front and the tails) in regimental colours. The turnbacks of the new coat had the same bugle horn badges as the previous *habit-long*. The *kinski* eventually started to be worn on all occasions except for parades (during which the *habit-long* continued to be used). Trumpeters wore the *kinski* in regimental colour and had white epaulettes, the mounted chasseurs of the Elite Companies having red epaulettes. The dress regulations of 1812 introduced the new *habit-veste* that was also prescribed for the dragoons and the lancers. This was basically identical to the previous *kinski*, except for having a plastron on the front. It was dark green and was piped in regimental colour. All ornaments and rank insignia remained the same as those worn on the previous *habit-long* and *kinski*. With the introduction of the *habit-veste*, the trumpeters were given the new Imperial Livery that has already been described for dragoons and lancers.

The mounted chasseurs wore dark green Hungarian breeches, having side-stripes and decorative embroidering ('Hungarian knots') on the front in regimental colour. The decorative knots had different shapes according to each regiment, but most of them were simple trefoils or bastion-shaped loops. The breeches showed rank, since those of officers consisted of more stripes of lace, the number of which corresponded to a specific rank. As an alternative to the tight Hungarian breeches, on campaign the mounted chasseurs could wear much more comfortable overalls: these were dark green and opened down the side by means of eighteen bone or pewter buttons along the outer seams. The inside leg and cuffs of these overalls were reinforced with black leather. By 1812, the overalls had been modified, receiving a front fly concealed by a flap and now having lace or piping in regimental colour on the length of the outer seams. Sometimes three-pointed flaps piped in regimental colour could be attached to the front of the garment. The boots used by the mounted chasseurs were of the classic Hungarian variety, with the top edge bordered with piping and having a frontal tassel in white (silver for officers). Belt equipment was white and all ranks wore wrist-length white gloves when riding.

The saddle-cloth consisted of a white half-shabraque (black for trumpeters) made of sheepskin, edged with small triangles of cloth in regimental colour, plus a dark green shabraque edged in regimental colour that had a regimental number in regimental colour on the back corner. Most of the superior officers had privately purchased exotic shabraques obtained from the skin of a leopard or tiger. The external edge of the officers' shabraques consisted of a different number of stripes of lace that corresponded to their rank.

The main weapon of the mounted chasseurs was the light cavalry sabre of the 'Year IV' model, which had a curved blade and hilt/scabbard fittings made of iron. Around 1807, this started to be replaced with the new 'Year IX' and 'Year XI' model sabres, which had an N-shaped copper basket guard and iron scabbard. Troopers and NCOs also carried a flintlock musketoon, which could be of the 1786 model or of the later 'Year IX' model. Trumpeters and officers did not have the musketoon, but instead carried a couple of flintlock pistols that could be of the old 1763 model or the newer 'Year XIII' model.

Chapter 7

The Artillery

History and organization

By the end of the eighteenth century, the artillery of the French Army was the best in Europe in terms of quantity as well as quality. In 1765, it had been completely reformed and modernized by the forward-thinking Lieutenant General Jean-Baptiste Vaquette de Gribeauval, who created a brand new artillery system that introduced lighter guns of more uniform calibre, which soon became known as the 'Gribeauval System'. The artillery pieces introduced after 1765 were one of the key factors behind the victories of the French armies of the Revolutionary and Napoleonic period. They were the result of a long scientific process that took place in the Age of Enlightenment and represented the most technologically advanced products that the French military apparatus was able to produce. Employed by competent and brilliant young officers like Napoleon, these weapons were more than a match for the other European armies. The central decades of the eighteenth century saw the development of mobile field artillery, with ballistics engineers and metallurgy technicians progressively reducing the weight of the gun barrels and designing lighter gun carriages. Calibres started to be standardized in order to ease the logistical problems that had previously been experienced, and new tactical theories were designed regarding the use of artillery on the battlefield. The guns of the eighteenth century were made of bronze – an alloy of ten parts copper to one part tin – and their methods of construction were constantly being improved. Until 1750, cannons were cast hollow around a core, which often moved within the mold, producing an imperfect bore. This problem was solved when the Dutch began casting their guns as a single solid block and then drilling the bore on a large machine designed for this specific task. All the European armies swiftly adopted this new construction system, which had numerous advantages: the new pieces had a better-aligned bore and tighter tolerances, along with less windage – i.e. the gap between the cannonball and the bore – and thus less gas pressure escaped so that smaller gunpowder charges could hurl a projectile further and more accurately than before. As a result of these improvements, cannon barrels started to be thinner, shorter and lighter.

Before 1765, France already possessed the only unified range of artillery in Europe, known as the 'Vallière System' after the name of its creator, who standardized guns from 4-pounders through to 24-pounders. Some traditionalist officers initially opposed the introduction of the new Gribeauval System, to the point that it became fully operative only in 1776. Eventually, however, the whole French artillery was re-equipped with the new and lighter pieces. The guns of the new system were approximately half the weight of those designed under the Vallière System, but had the same range. The Gribeauval System prescribed the use of three different kinds of cannons and of one kind of howitzer for field artillery: 12-pounder, 8-pounder and 4-pounder cannons and 6-inch howitzers. These all had new standardized carriages, built with interchangeable parts, which were lighter and narrower than the previous ones. The carriages had two positions for the trunnions: a forward position for firing and a rear position for transport. The draft horses started to be harnessed in pairs rather than in single file, and all the pieces were fitted with a rear-calibrated gunsight as well as with an elevating screw. The new quick-match tubes introduced by Gribeauval generated a better ignition of the gunpowder charges, which started to be placed inside pre-packaged flannel bags. A new vent-pricker, a special tool used to make a hole in the gunpowder bags, thus came into use. For siege and garrison artillery, Gribeauval retained the calibres introduced by Vallière in 1732 but improved the pieces as described above. Four kinds of guns were used by the French siege and garrison artillery: 24-pounder and 16-pounder cannons, and 12-pounder and 8-pounder siege cannons. Gribeauval also designed a range of mortars, which were mostly used for bombarding static positions, in the following calibres: 12-inch, short 10-inch, long 10-inch and 8-inch. Napoleon did not modify the Gribeauval System in a significant way during his reign, although in 1805 he replaced the 4-pounder and 8-pounder cannons with the new 6-pounder 'Year XI' field gun. The 6-inch howitzer, meanwhile, was replaced with the new 'Year XI' 24-pounder howitzer.

Even before the outbreak of the Revolution, the French artillery had competent officers who did not come – at least for the major part – from the aristocratic families of the country. These men, including the young Napoleon, underwent a modern training that made them capable of using the pieces of the Gribeauval System in a very effective way. The artillery officers thus had scientific and technological skills that were unparalleled in the French Army, having spent several years studying the latest improvements in the 'art of the artillery' and earned their promotions only thanks to their personal capabilities. The artillery was the most modern and least aristocratic of the French Army's branches of service. As a result, when many royalist officers left their military units after the start of the French Revolution, it was not seriously damaged like the infantry or the cavalry. In 1791, the French artillery consisted of seven foot regiments, each of which comprised two battalions with ten companies/batteries each. During the turbulent years of the Revolutionary Wars, several units of volunteer or National Guard artillery were formed, but these were made up of inexperienced soldiers who were not capable of manning their pieces effectively. Consequently, the French authorities decided to disband all the volunteer/National Guard artillery units in 1796 and to use their best members to form a new regiment of regular foot artillery. Meanwhile, as was the case with other European armies, the new horse artillery was being created thanks to the introduction of the lighter guns designed by Gribeauval. The first two 'flying batteries' of the French Army were established in 1791 by General Mathieu Dumas, although these had their gunners still riding on caissons rather than on horseback. In April 1792, nine companies of horse artillery were formed, three of which were fully mounted on horses. Recruited from the foot artillery and the infantry grenadiers, these were not expert horsemen but soon became famous for their combat skills. Each of these early mounted artillery companies comprised four officers, eleven NCOs, three artificers, two trumpeters and sixty gunners. In February 1794, following the success of the early horse artillery companies, the mounted branch was enlarged to comprise nine regiments (later reduced to eight) with six companies/batteries each. The new units were mostly recruited from cavalrymen, who had limited artillery skills but an incredible enthusiasm.

By the end of 1799, when Napoleon became First Consul, the artillery of the French Army comprised eight foot regiments with twenty companies each and eight horse regiments of six companies each. These were supplemented by an Artillery General Staff consisting of 266 officers, twelve companies of *ouvriers* (artillery workers) and two pontoon battalions. In 1801, the number of horse artillery regiments was reduced to six and that of the artillery workers' companies was increased to 15. A single company/battery of foot artillery consisted of the following elements: one first captain, one second captain, one first lieutenant, one second lieutenant, one sergeant-major, four sergeants, one fourrier, four corporals, two drummers, twenty-one workers/artificers and seventy-seven gunners (later reduced to sixty-eight). Each company/battery of horse artillery comprised the following: one first captain, one second captain, one first lieutenant, one second lieutenant, one sergeant-major, four sergeants, one fourrier, four corporals, two trumpeters, eight workers/artificers and fifty-nine gunners. Throughout the Napoleonic period, it was usual for each foot company to have six cannons and two howitzers and for each horse company to have four guns (usually 6-pounders) and two howitzers. Each battery was a self-contained entity with its own train and thus could serve independently. In 1810, following the disbandment of the Dutch Army, a new regiment of foot artillery and one of horse artillery were organized with former members of the Dutch artillery, although the mounted unit was soon dissolved. From 1811, the number of companies in each foot artillery regiment was progressively enlarged, reaching twenty-eight by 1813, whereas each of the horse regiments received an additional depot company after 1809. In addition to the foot and horse artillery regiments, there were also the armourers (one company in 1803, increased to two in 1805) and the *ouvriers*, who were structured on eighteen companies by 1813. A single company of armourers consisted of four officers and sixty-eight privates, while a company of artillery workers comprised five officers and 149 privates. With the first restoration of the Bourbons in 1814, the foot artillery was reduced to eight regiments with sixteen companies each and the horse artillery to four regiments of four companies. In addition to these there were twelve companies of *ouvriers* and a pontoon battalion.

Initially, the foot artillery relied upon civilian transport-drivers hired from private contractors for moving its guns, who – though being exposed to the dangers of the battlefield – were not subject to military discipline and were usually neglected by their employers. In 1800, Napoleon decided to militarize the artillery drivers by transforming them into soldiers. This change had very positive consequences, since instead of being unharnessed at the edge of the battlefield and then being dragged into action by the gunners, the pieces were now positioned into the heart of the action by the artillery drivers. Eight battalions of the Artillery Train were formed in 1800, one for each of the existing foot artillery regiments, consisting of one elite and four line companies each. A single company comprised seven NCOs and sixty privates. The soldiers of the train were distributed amongst the artillery batteries and had no officers, since they were commanded by the battery officers. In 1801, the elite company was abolished and the number of companies in each battalion was increased to six. By 1808, there were thirteen battalions of the Artillery Train, but this number was doubled in 1810 with the formation of 'bis' units and a 14th Battalion was also raised from former members of the Dutch Army. With the restoration of 1814, the Artillery Train was reorganized on four squadrons with fifteen officers and 271 men each, but these were doubled to eight squadrons by Napoleon for the Belgian campaign of 1815.

Regimental artillery or 'battalion guns' were a common feature in the late eighteenth century, it being common practice to include some artillery pieces within the line infantry units. These light guns, crewed by infantrymen, were tasked with providing immediate fire support for the foot regiments and battalions. The French line infantry included some light pieces until January 1798, when they were abolished. In June

Officer of the foot artillery with pre-1812 uniform.

The Artillery 93

Gunners of the foot artillery with pre-1812 dress.

1809, the emperor, having at his disposal large amounts of captured guns that had been taken from defeated enemies, reintroduced the concept of regimental artillery and assigned two light cannons plus a platoon of twenty-two gunners, along with two platoons of twenty artillery drivers, to several of his line/light infantry regiments.

This 'regimental artillery', however, was quite short-lived, being completely destroyed during the Russian campaign.

In addition to the foot artillery and horse artillery, the French Army also included another three categories of artillery: the Coast Artillery, the Garrison Artillery and the Veteran Artillery. The Coast Artillery was tasked with manning the shore fortifications of France and consisted of 100 independent companies of Cannoniers-

Gunners and officer of the foot artillery with M1812 uniform.

Gardes-Cotes. These were gradually expanded by Napoleon, reaching a total of 144 by 1812, but with the first restoration of the Bourbons, the Cannoniers-Gardes-Cotes were disbanded. The Garrison Artillery was tasked with manning the many fortifications that were located on French territory and consisted of twenty-eight independent companies of Cannoniers Sédentaires (augmented to thirty by 1812). The Veteran Artillery was part of a larger corps formed in 1792 and known as 'Invalid Companies', which was made up of old soldiers who were no longer able to perform active duties. In 1799, the Veteran Artillery within the Invalid Companies consisted of thirteen independent companies with fifty-two gunners each. There were nineteen companies of Veteran Artillery by 1812, a figure reduced to ten with the first restoration of the Bourbons.

Uniforms and equipment

The French foot artillery always dressed quite similarly to the line infantry, its uniforms remaining almost unchanged until 1812. Being dark blue with red facings, they were very easy to recognize on the battlefield. In 1799, the foot artillerymen wore a black bicorn with national cockade having an orange-yellow lace holder and red pompom made of wool, and a dark blue long-tailed coat with brass buttons and dark blue frontal lapels piped in red, dark blue shoulder straps piped in red, dark blue collar piped in red, red round cuffs, dark blue cuff flaps piped in red, red turnbacks adorned with dark blue flaming grenade badges, and horizontal pocket flaps on the back of the tails piped in red and having three buttons. They also wore a dark blue waistcoat, dark blue trousers, black gaiters during cold months or white gaiters during hot months, and black shoes. During the Napoleonic period, only a few features of their uniform were slightly modified: the tails of the coat became shorter in order to be more practical and the frontal lapels started to have an accentuated curve. The black bicorn hat was worn in two different positions according to the activities that its wearer was performing: when worn across the head (*en bataille*) its wearer was ready to fight; when worn fore-and-aft (*en colonne*) its wearer was marching. The foot artillerymen, as an alternative to the bicorn, could have the *bonnet de police* undress cap, which was dark blue with red piping and had a tasselled stocking end folded up and tucked behind the right-hand side of a stiffened headband. The tassel was red and on the front of the cap there was a red flaming grenade.

According to the egalitarian principles of the French Revolution, officers were dressed exactly like their men but their uniforms were of finer material. The lace holder of the bicorn's cockade was golden for officers, who also wore a gilt gorget under their neck. This was mostly used on parade and incorporated a decorative silver device that depicted a flaming grenade placed above two crossed cannons. The gorget was the last remnant of the medieval knight's armour, a symbol of high military status. Officers showed rank on their uniforms with gold lace epaulettes that were worn on the shoulders, these being designed according to a general scheme that had been introduced in 1786 and remained valid after the outbreak of the revolution. NCOs' ranks were indicated by diagonal bars of lace applied on the lower sleeves: two orange-yellow bars for corporals, one golden bar piped in red for sergeants and two golden bars piped in red for sergeant-majors. Both NCOs and rankers had lace service chevrons on the left upper sleeves of their coats, which were worn point uppermost and were golden for senior NCOs or red for junior NCOs and rankers. The number of inverted chevrons corresponded to the years of service: one for ten years of service, two for fifteen years and three for twenty years.

In February 1806, an important modification was made to the uniforms of the French foot artillery, the bicorn being replaced with a shako. The new shako headgear had a body made of black felt or board, which widened slightly towards the top, and a waterproofed crown. Around the top and bottom of the shako there were reinforcing leather bands, while on the front there was a leather peak. A leather chevron was usually applied as strengthening on each side of the headgear. On the front of the top band there was a tricolour cockade placed above a lozenge-shaped brass plate that bore an embossed imperial eagle placed above two crossed cannons and a regimental number. The shako was kept in position by brass chinscales that consisted of circular bosses; the first boss on each side, applied on the bottom band of the headgear, was larger than the others and bore a decorative badge (a flaming grenade). Above the cockade there was a red woollen pompom, which could be surmounted by a red plume when worn with parade dress. Wrapped around the shako there were red decorative cords and flounders, which were usually removed while on campaign. The shakos of the officers had gold lace on the top band, golden cords/flounders, golden lace holder for the cockade and gilded fittings.

On 19 January 1812, new dress regulations were announced for the French Army, which remained in use until the final fall of Napoleon in 1815. Named after Major Bardin, who was responsible for their issue, these regulations retained the general features and colours of the current foot artillery uniform, but introduced some important modifications. For instance, the old coat was replaced with a double-breasted and short-tailed dark blue jacket known as a *habit-veste*. This new jacket had dark blue plastron-style lapels piped in red on the front and vertical pockets on the back. Rank distinctions and service chevrons remained unchanged. The dark blue waistcoat, which was no longer visible, now had a lower collar and coloured shoulder straps. The black or white gaiters no longer extended over the knee. The 1812 dress regulations also introduced a new model of shako, with a new kind of brass frontal plate that bore a crowned imperial eagle atop a semi-circular plate into which the regimental number was cut. The new shako had decorative brass finials that reproduced a flaming grenade. The usual tricolour cockade and brass chinscales of the previous model of shako were retained, and although cords and flounders were officially abolished, in practice they continued to be worn by most of the regiments. The new shako had a red tufted pompom on the front. The Bardin Regulations introduced a new model of fatigue cap that replaced the *bonnet de police*, known as the *pokalem*, a pie-shaped dark blue cap with a folding neck-flap that could be fastened under the chin. The *pokalem* was piped in red and bore a red flaming grenade on the front.

The uniforms of the foot artillery musicians were governed, until the 1812 dress regulations, by the personal tastes of the colonels commanding the individual regiments. Members of the regimental band wore coats in extravagant colours (red in most cases), which sometimes had an exotic flavour and were frequently used together with non-regulation headgear such as bicorn hats adorned with ostrich-feathers or Polish czapkas. The uniforms of the regimental bandsmen were a riot of colour: their facings were all trimmed with multi-coloured lace, they had trefoil-shaped epaulettes in the same colour as their trimming and sometimes included decorative shoulder wings. Trousers could be decorated on the front with embroidered knots, while the standard footwear was usually replaced with black leather half-boots having coloured top edging and frontal tassel. Plumes, pompoms, cords and flounders of the shakos could be in many different colours (usually matching that of the coat or those of the trimming). The musicians of individual companies/batteries were dressed in a much simpler way and looked more or less like their comrades. They had coloured lacing on the facings, pockets and turnbacks, and usually had decorative stripes of coloured lace applied on the sleeves and coloured shoulder-wings. Shako ornaments, company distinctions, badges on the turnbacks and epaulettes were all the same as the ordinary gunners. The Bardin Regulations tried to regularize the uniforms of the musicians by introducing a standard Imperial Livery to be worn by all. This consisted of a dark green single-breasted jacket decorated with stripes of lace having alternate yellow and green segments. The yellow segments were decorated with an interwoven dark green crowned 'N', the dark green segments with an interwoven yellow imperial eagle. During the brief restoration of the Bourbons in 1814, some elements of the foot artillery uniform were modified, the tricolour cockade being replaced with a royal white one and a new shako plate bearing the coat-of-arms of the royal family coming into use.

The French horse artillery was always dressed quite similarly to the cavalry's mounted chasseurs, but in dark blue with red facings. Until 1803, the headgear of the mounted artillery was a shako of the mirliton type, which was characterized by the presence of a *flamme*/turban that was wrapped around its body and by a detachable peak on its front. This early shako was 19cm in height and 22cm in diameter, and had a red plume and tricolour cockade on the left side. The *flamme* of the mirliton was red, while the main body of the shako was black. Red cords and flounders were frequently wrapped around the headgear, together with the turban. In 1803, a new model of shako was introduced after the following modifications were made: both the *flamme* and detachable peak were removed, the cockade and plume were moved to the front of the headgear and a plate was added beneath the cockade. The brass plate was lozenge-shaped and bore the regimental number together with two crossed cannons. The shako was maintained in place by a strap that passed beneath the wearer's queue. In 1805/06, the headgear was slightly modified in its shape, becoming taller and more bell-shaped, while its strap was replaced by brass chinscales. As a result of these changes, a new model of shako came into use in 1806. Decorative cords and flounders, although redundant, continued to be worn with this new version of the headgear. On 9 November 1810, the use of these cords and flounders was officially abolished and the red plume worn on the front of the headgear was replaced by a simple lentil-shaped pompom made of wool. These modifications, however, were never particularly popular and were thus introduced only very slowly. Like for the mounted chasseurs, officers and trumpeters frequently had a black colpack with red plume and bag instead of the standard shako. The new shako introduced in 1812 for the foot artillery was also given to the horse artillery. This had a frontal plate consisting of a crescent (bearing the unit number) surmounted by an imperial eagle. Off-duty, all horse artillerymen wore the standard *bonnet de police* fatigue cap in dark blue with piping and frontal tassel in red, which was replaced after 1812 by the new *pokalem* headgear. Both the *bonnet de police* and *pokalem* had the distinctive flaming grenade of the artillery embroidered in red on the front. Officers used their own versions of the headgear described above, having golden top bands for the shakos and golden cords and flounders for the colpacks.

Up until 1811, the mounted artillerymen wore a hussar-style uniform that comprised a dolman but not a pelisse. The dolman was dark blue with a standing collar piped in red and red pointed cuffs. It was fastened along its entire length by between thirteen and eighteen semi-circular pewter buttons and red braid loops. The jacket had three rows of buttons on the front, and its waist, back-seams and front vent were piped in red. The jackets of the officers were almost identical to

The Artillery 99

Trumpeter (left) and troopers (right) of the mounted artillery wearing busby and dolman.

those of the NCOs/rankers, but had five rows of buttons instead of three and their frogging/piping was golden rather than red. Rank was shown by yellow inverted chevrons applied above the pointed cuffs of the dolman, these chevrons being golden for officers. Years of service for troopers/NCOs were shown by red inverted chevrons applied on the left sleeve. Trumpeters had dolmans in red with facings in dark blue. In 1811, the dolman was replaced by the *habit-long*, which had been worn until then

Officer of the mounted artillery wearing shako and dolman.

The Artillery 101

Trooper of the mounted artillery wearing shako and dolman.

Troopers of the mounted artillery wearing pre-1812 shako and *habit-long*.

as campaign dress. This consisted of a long-tailed and lapelled tunic that had the same colouring as the dolman jacket except for the following particulars: the dark blue tails of the skirt were turned back to reveal their red lining and their turnbacks were adorned with a dark blue flaming grenade device, and the frontal lapels were dark blue with red piping. The new tunic had red epaulettes, and on the back of the tails there were false vertical pockets with three buttons each that were piped in red. The officers' rank was now shown by golden epaulettes worn on the shoulders. Under the *habit-long*, the mounted artillerymen wore a sleeveless waistcoat, which was single-breasted and was supposed to be dark blue. Quite frequently, however, this item of dress was in red and was double-breasted instead of single-breasted. The waistcoat had red frontal frogging like the old dolman. Trumpeters wore the *habit-long* with reversed colours and had white epaulettes.

From 1811, a simple single-breasted coat known as a *kinski* came into use for campaign dress. This was dark blue and had standing collar, pointed cuffs and short tails, and being designed for campaign use, was very practical to wear. The *kinski* had collar and cuffs like those of the *habit-long* and was piped (on the front and the tails) in red. The turnbacks of the new coat had the same flaming grenade badges as the previous *habit-long*. The *kinski* slowly started to be worn on all occasions except for parades (during which the *habit-long* continued to be used). Trumpeters wore the *kinski* in red and had white epaulettes. The dress regulations of 1812 introduced the new *habit-veste*, which was also prescribed for the foot artillery, this being basically identical to the previous *kinski* except for having a plastron on the front. The *habit-veste* was dark blue and was piped in red. All ornaments and rank insigna remained the same as those worn on the previous *habit-long*. With the introduction of the new *habit-veste*, trumpeters were given the new Imperial Livery that has already been described for the foot artillery. The horse artillerymen wore dark blue Hungarian breeches, with side-stripes and decorative embroidering on the front – known as Hungarian knots – in red. The decorative knots were trefoil-shaped until 1812 and then bastion-shaped; they showed rank, since those of officers consisted of more stripes of lace and the number of the latter corresponded to a specific rank. As an alternative to the tight Hungarian breeches, on campaign the mounted artillerymen could wear much more comfortable overalls, which were dark blue and opened down the side by means of eighteen bone or pewter buttons along the outer seams. The inside leg and cuffs of these overalls were reinforced with black leather. By 1812, the overalls had been modified, receiving a front fly concealed by a flap and now having lace or piping in red on the length of the outer seams. Three-pointed flaps piped in red could be attached to the front of the garment. The boots used by the horse artillerymen were of the classic Hungarian variety, with the top edge bordered with piping and a frontal tassel in yellow (golden for officers). Belt equipment was white and all ranks wore wrist-length white gloves when riding. The saddle-cloth consisted of a white sheepskin half-shabraque (black for trumpeters) that was edged with small triangles of red cloth, and a dark blue shabraque edged in red that had a red flaming grenade on the back corner. Most of the superior officers had their own exotic shabraques made from the skin of a leopard or tiger. The external edge of the officers' shabraques consisted of a different number of stripes of lace that corresponded to their rank. Like the hussars, the horse artillerymen had a *sabretache* and barrel-sash in dark blue and red.

The *ouvriers* or artillery workers, the armourers and the pontoniers were dressed exactly like the foot artillerymen, as were the Garrison Artillery and Veteran Artillery. The *Cannoniers-Gardes-Cotes*, however, had a peculiar dress. Until 1810,

Troopers and trumpeter of the mounted artillery with M1812 uniform.

Private of the Cannoniers garde-côte with pre-1810 uniform.

this consisted of the following elements: black bicorn with tricolour national cockade having orange-yellow lace holder, red pompom and red tuft, a white coat with medium blue collar, round cuffs, cuff flaps, frontal lapels and turnbacks, red epaulettes, a white waistcoat, white trousers, black gaiters and black shoes. In 1810,

Private of the Cannoniers garde-côte with M1810 dress.

the following new uniform was introduced: black shako with tricolour national cockade, red pompom, red tuft and brass frontal plate showing an anchor over two crossed cannons, a dark blue coat with green collar, round cuffs, cuff flaps, frontal lapels and turnbacks, red epaulettes, a green waistcoat, green trousers, black stockings and black shoes. On the turnbacks of the coat there were decorative flaming grenade badges, in medium blue for the first model of coat and in dark blue for that introduced in 1810.

The first uniform given to the Artillery Train was as follows: black bicorn with tricolour national cockade having orange-yellow lace holder and coloured tuft (half iron grey and half red), an iron grey coat with dark blue collar, round cuffs, frontal lapels and turnbacks, iron grey shoulder straps piped in dark blue, a white waistcoat, white breeches and black boots. In 1807, the bicorn was replaced with the shako, and in 1808, the main colour of the uniform was changed. In consequence, the new dress of the Artillery Train now featured a black shako with sky blue frontal plume, cords and flounders, a tricolour national cockade with sky blue lace holder, sky blue pompom with red central part bearing unit number in white metal, white metal chinscale and white metal frontal plate bearing an Imperial Eagle above unit number. They also wore a sky blue coat with dark blue collar, round cuffs and frontal lapels piped in sky blue, sky blue cuff flaps piped in dark blue, dark blue turnbacks and sky blue shoulder straps piped in dark blue, along with a sky blue waistcoat, white breeches and black leather boots. The new sky blue colour of the tunic, in most cases, was practically identical to the previous iron grey. In 1810, the coat was replaced with a simpler single-breasted *surtout* of the same colour, having dark blue collar, cuffs and turnbacks all piped in white. This was usually worn together with sky blue overalls having side-buttons and leather reinforcements, which had been popular since the creation of the Artillery Train. In 1812, they were given the new *habit-veste* – in iron grey, not sky blue – and the new brass plate for the shako. As a result, the uniform of the Artillery Train became as follows: black shako with tricolour national cockade, red pompom, white metal chinscale and white metal frontal plate bearing an Imperial Eagle above a crescent with unit number, an iron grey *habit-veste* with dark blue collar, round cuffs, frontal plastron and short turnbacks, iron grey cuff flaps and shoulder straps piped in dark blue, iron grey flaming grenade badges on the turnbacks, white breeches or iron grey overalls and black leather boots. Until 1812, the musicians of the Artillery Train were dressed in uniforms with reversed colours, then with the new dress regulations of that year they were given the Imperial Livery. Belt equipment was white and all ranks wore white leather gauntlet-like gloves. The saddle-cloth consisted of a white sheepskin half-shabraque edged with small triangles of dark blue cloth, and an iron grey shabraque edged in white that had a white flaming grenade on the back corner.

Private of the Artillery Train with pre-1812 uniform.

The Artillery 109

Private of the Artillery Train with M1812 dress and *bonnet de police*.

Trumpeter of the Artillery Train with pre-1812 uniform.

Chapter 8

The Technical Corps

History and organization

In 1789, the French Army contained a small staff of engineer officers plus six companies of sappers and six companies of miners, which despite being small from a numerical point of view, were well regarded and were part – at least formally – of the artillery. The engineer officers were extremely competent, and with coming from the same middle-class families as the artillery officers, they did not suffer from the exiling of aristocratic officers after the outbreak of the French Revolution. In 1793, the country's new republican government assembled the engineer officers, miners and sappers into an independent Engineer Corps, the miners continuing to consist of six companies, while the sappers were increased to nine battalions with eight companies in each. In 1798, the sappers were reduced to four battalions and later, during 1799, to just two battalions, having 1,800 men each. A single company of sappers at this time comprised the following elements: four officers, nine NCOs, four artisans, one drummer and forty-eight privates. By 1806, the number of privates had been increased to 154. During the same year, the Engineer Train was established, which was organized as a single battalion with seven companies in 1811. In 1808, the miners were restructured on two battalions with five companies each (later increased to six), while in 1811, an independent company of engineer workers (*ouvriers*) was formed. Meanwhile, the number of sapper battalions was progressively expanded, so that by 1812 there was a total of eight such units. After 1809, the staff of engineer officers was supplemented by a small corps of Geographical Engineers, consisting of ninety officers who were tasked with producing accurate maps for the army. The French sappers were supported in their activities by several labour battalions recruited from PoWs, which were rarely employed on the battlefield: *Compagnies de Pionniers*, independent companies formed from conscripts who had mutilated themselves to avoid military service; *Pionniers Blancs*, two battalions formed from PoWs; and *Pionniers Espagnols*, four companies formed from Spanish PoWs interned in France after their country left the alliance with Napoleon to side with Great Britain.

During the early Napoleonic period, all the materials of the French Army were transported by civilian contractors, but the emperor was never particularly happy with

Drummer of the engineers with pre-1812 dress.

The Technical Corps 113

Private of the engineers with M1812 uniform.

Private of the engineers with M1812 dress and the white cockade that was briefly worn on the shako during the first restoration of the Bourbons (1814).

the services provided by these private citizens, who were often prone to corruption. As a result, in 1807, Napoleon decided to militarize the civilian transporters by creating the Train of the Equipments. This initially consisted of eight battalions with four companies each, a single battalion being equipped with 140 waggons. Four waggons in each company were used as ambulances, while the remainder were allocated either to individual units to carry their provisions or to a centralized train that was tasked with transporting reserve rations/munitions. The Train of the Equipments was greatly expanded over a number of years, reaching an establishment of twenty-one battalions by 1812, one of these consisting entirely of medical vehicles. After the calamitous Russian campaign, the number of battalions was temporarily reduced to nine, but was later increased to twelve. Each battalion of the Train of the Equipments had a staff comprising four officers, five NCOs and five craftsmen. A single company consisted of the following elements: one sub-lieutenant, seven NCOs, four craftsmen and eighty drivers. From 1812, the Train of the Equipments also comprised two battalions of workers or *ouvriers*.

Uniforms and equipment

The French engineer officers, sappers and miners were always dressed quite similarly to the foot artillery, but with facings in black. In 1799, the uniform included a black bicorn with national cockade having orange-yellow lace holder and red pompom made of wool (this was half-red and half-black for miners), and a dark blue long-tailed coat with brass buttons and black frontal lapels piped in red, dark blue shoulder straps piped in red, black collar piped in red, black round cuffs piped in red, black cuff flaps piped in red, red turnbacks adorned with dark blue flaming grenade badges, horizontal pocket flaps on the back of the tails piped in red and having three buttons. They also wore a dark blue waistcoat, dark blue trousers, black gaiters during cold months or white gaiters during hot months, and black shoes. Over time, some features of this uniform were slightly modified, with the tails of the coat being shortened in order to be more practical and the frontal lapels starting to have an accentuated curve. All the engineers, as an alternative to the bicorn, could use the *bonnet de police* undress cap, which was dark blue with red piping and had a tasselled stocking end folded up and tucked behind the right-hand side of a stiffened headband. The tassel was red, and on the front of the cap there was a red badge consisting of two crossed axes. Officers were dressed exactly like their men, but their uniforms were of finer material. The lace holder of the bicorn's cockade was golden for officers, who also wore a gilt gorget under their neck. The gorget was mostly used on parade and incorporated a decorative silver device showing two crossed axes.

Officers showed rank on their uniforms with gold lace epaulettes that were worn on the shoulders. NCOs' ranks were shown by diagonal bars of lace that were applied on the lower sleeves: two orange-yellow bars for corporals, one golden bar piped in red for sergeants and two golden bars piped in red for sergeant-majors. Both NCOs and rankers had lace service chevrons on the left upper sleeves of their coats, which were worn point uppermost and were golden for senior NCOs or red for junior NCOs and rankers.

In 1806, the bicorn was replaced with the shako. This had a body made of black felt or board, which widened slightly towards the top, and a waterproofed crown. Around the top and the bottom of the shako there were leather bands in red that reinforced it, while on the front there was a leather peak. A red leather chevron was applied as strengthening on each side of the headgear. On the front of the top band there was a tricolour cockade placed above a lozenge-shaped brass plate that bore an embossed imperial eagle placed above the unit number. The shako was kept in place by brass chinscales that consisted of circular bosses, the first boss on each side, applied on the bottom band of the headgear, being larger than the others. Above the cockade there was a red woollen pompom (half-red and half-black for miners), surmounted by a small tuft of the same colour. Wrapped around the shako there were red decorative cords and flounders, which were usually removed while on campaign. The shakos of the officers had gold lace on the top band, golden cords/flounders, golden lace holder for the cockade and gilded fittings.

The new dress regulations of 1812 retained the general features and colours of the previous engineer uniform, but introduced some important modifications, the old coat being replaced by a double-breasted and short-tailed dark blue jacket known as a *habit-veste*. The *habit-veste* had black plastron-style lapels piped in red on the front and vertical pockets on the back. Rank distinctions and service chevrons remained unchanged. The dark blue waistcoat, which was no longer visible, now had a lower collar and coloured shoulder straps. The black or white gaiters no longer extended over the knee. The 1812 dress regulations introduced a new model of shako, with a new kind of brass frontal plate that bore a crowned imperial eagle atop a semi-circular plate, into which the unit number was cut. The usual tricolour cockade and brass chinscales of the previous model of shako were retained. Cords and flounders were officially abolished, but in practice they continued to be worn by most of the regiments. The new shako had a red tufted pompom on the front (half-red and half-black for miners). The 1812 regulations also introduced a new model of fatigue cap that replaced the *bonnet de police* with the *pokalem*, a pie-shaped dark blue cap with a folding neck-flap that could be fastened under the chin. The *pokalem* was piped in red and had a red badge consisting of two crossed axes on the front. During the

Private (left) and trumpeter (right) of the Train of the Equipments with pre-1812 dress.

brief restoration of the Bourbons in 1814, some elements of the engineer uniform were modified, with the tricolour cockade replaced by a royal white one and a new shako plate bearing the coat-of-arms of the royal family coming into use. The train of the Engineer Corps was dressed like the Artillery Train in iron grey, but with black facings instead of dark blue.

The 1807 uniform of the Train of the Equipments included a black shako with brown pompom, half-red and half-brown plume, brown cords and flounders, tricolour

Private of the Train of the Equipments with pre-1812 uniform.

The Technical Corps

Private of the Train of the Equipments with M1812 dress.

national cockade with brown lace holder, white metal chinscale and white metal frontal plate bearing an imperial eagle above unit number, and an iron grey coat with brown collar and frontal lapels piped in iron grey, brown pointed cuffs, brown turnbacks, iron grey shoulder straps piped in brown and iron grey five-pointed star badges on the turnbacks. There was also a white waistcoat, white breeches and black leather boots. On campaign, the breeches were replaced with iron grey overalls that had side-buttons and leather reinforcements, which were quite popular. In 1812, the Train of the Equipments was also given the new *habit-veste* and the new brass plate for the shako its uniform thus comprising a black shako with tricolour national cockade, brown pompom, white metal chinscale and white metal frontal plate bearing an imperial eagle above a crescent with the unit number, and an iron grey *habit-veste* with brown collar, round cuffs, frontal plastron and short turnbacks, iron grey cuff flaps and shoulder straps piped in brown and iron grey five-pointed star badges on the turnbacks. Its members also wore white breeches or iron grey overalls and black leather boots. Until 1812, the musicians of the Train of the Equipments were dressed with uniforms having reversed colours, then with the new dress regulations of that year, they were given the Imperial Livery. Belt equipment was white and all ranks wore white leather gauntlet-like gloves. The saddle-cloth comprised a white half-shabraque made of sheepskin that was edged with small triangles of brown cloth, plus an iron grey shabraque edged in white.

Chapter 9

The Security Corps

On 16 February 1791, the new revolutionary government of France decided to reform the police of its country, disbanding the old Maréchaussée Royale (Royal Constabulary), which was extremely loyal to the king and thus could not continue serving under the new regime. In place of the Royal Constabulary, a new Gendarmerie Nationale (National Gendarmerie) was created, a highly militarized police corps tasked with enforcing the application of laws in every large city or small village of France. By 1801, the Gendarmerie was structured on twenty-six territorial legions, each of which was stationed in a different department of France. A single legion, depending on the extent and population of its home territory, comprised a different number of detachments or brigades. These could be foot or mounted units, since the French Gendarmerie consisted of both. In 1801, following a reorganization ordered by Napoleon, the Gendarmerie comprised a total of 750 foot brigades and 1,750 mounted brigades. Each brigade consisted of one commanding NCO and five policemen. On 17 November 1804, the French Gendarmerie received the new denomination of Gendarmerie Impériale, or Imperial Gendarmerie, and each of its legions was restructured on two squadrons. With the expansion of the French Empire, several new legions of gendarmes were created in the territories that were conquered by Napoleon. Indeed, the Gendarmerie played a prominent role in cracking down on anti-French political activities as well as in keeping order in the most turbulent areas of the empire. Two new legions were created for northern Italy, one for Tuscany, one for Rome, one for the Illyrian provinces and three for the Netherlands, meaning that by 1811, the Imperial Gendarmerie comprised a total of thirty-four legions.

After conquering Spain, Napoleon soon realized that its population would never be prepared to submit to the French through peaceful means. The Spanish civilians, in fact, rose up in rebellion against the invaders and started to conduct a series of irregular military operations that are collectively known as the guerrilla. To counter the activities of the Spanish insurgents, who were extremely effective and numerous, the emperor had no choice but to use many of his regular military units, plus hundreds of gendarmes. The gendarmes were specifically trained to conduct counter-guerrilla operations and to control the civilians who could potentially become insurgents. On 24 November 1809, Napoleon decided to create a separate branch of his Imperial

Trooper of the Mounted Gendarmerie wearing bicorn.

The Security Corps   123

Trooper of the Gendarmerie of Spain wearing shako.

Gendarmerie to serve in Spain and fight against the *guerrilleros*: the Gendarmerie Française d'Espagne (French Gendarmerie of Spain). Twenty mounted squadrons were tasked with a series of auxiliary duties that were fundamental for the functioning of the French Army in Spain: chasing insurgents, escorting convoys, transporting messages and controlling the civilian population. The gendarmes of the new corps were recruited from veteran policemen and soldiers, and were thus experienced fighters. Each squadron of the Gendarmerie Française d'Espagne was a mixed force of infantry and cavalry, comprising four mounted officers, five foot officers, ten mounted NCOs, ten foot NCOs, seventy mounted gendarmes and 110 foot gendarmes. The mounted gendarmes were all equipped with cavalry lances and were trained to intercept the Spanish *guerrilleros* on every kind of terrain thanks to their high degree of mobility. The French Gendarmerie of Spain was disbanded in 1814 after the French Army was forced out of Spain by British troops under Wellington and their Spanish and Portuguese allies.

During the Napoleonic Wars, the Imperial Gendarmerie, despite not being part of the French Army, performed a series of important non-combat functions that were vital for the success of Napoleon's campaigns, from guarding prisoners and providing escorts and couriers, to gathering information from civilians and keeping order among the ranks of the military units as a sort of military police.

Uniforms and Equipment

The foot gendarmes were uniformed as follows: black bicorn with national cockade, white edging and red plume, a dark blue coat with dark blue collar piped in red and red round cuffs, dark blue cuff flaps piped in red, red frontal lapels, red epaulettes and red turnbacks, a buff waistcoat and trousers, black leggings and shoes, and buff leather belt equipment. On campaign, the plume of the bicorn was removed, the coat was replaced by a dark blue single-breasted *surtout* with red frontal piping and the trousers were also dark blue. The drummers of the foot gendarmes were dressed like the ordinary policemen, but with uniforms in reversed colours (red with dark blue facings). The mounted gendarmes wore the following uniform: black bicorn with national cockade, white edging and red plume, a dark blue coat with dark blue collar piped in red and red round cuffs, dark blue cuff flaps piped in red, red frontal lapels, white contre-epaulettes and white aiguillettes on the left shoulder, buff leather gauntlet-like gloves, buff waistcoat and trousers, black leather boots and buff leather belt equipment. The shabraque was dark blue with white external edging and white flaming grenade embroidered on the back corner. On campaign, the mounted gendarmes' coat was replaced by a dark blue single-breasted *surtout* with red frontal piping, which was worn together with dark grey overalls. The trumpeters of the mounted gendarmes were dressed like the other policemen, but with uniforms in reversed colours (red with dark blue facings), while the collar, cuffs and frontal lapels of their coats were piped in white on the external edges and buttonholes. All members of the Gendarmerie had a dark blue *bonnet de police*, with white piping and frontal tassel, which was worn in barracks. In 1812, the uniforms described above were slightly modified, the coats being replaced by the new *habit-veste* that had their same colouring but a red plastron on the front. The Gendarmerie Française d'Espagne had its foot members uniformed like the ordinary foot gendarmes, while its mounted members were dressed with the same shako, *habit-long* and Hungarian breeches as the mounted chasseurs (in dark blue with red facings).

The Paris Guard

Paris had always had a special guard corps acting both as the garrison of the city and as an urban police that was tasked with keeping order in the capital. In 1789, the Paris Guard sided with the revolutionaries and was thus retained in service by the new government, but two years later it was disbanded following the general reorganization of the Gendarmerie. With the creation and the expansion of the National Guard, which counted several units in Paris, for some years the French capital did not have an independent corps of militarized police. This situation came to an end in 1802, when First Consul Napoleon decided to create a strong corps of militarized policemen who could keep order in his capital. Paris, especially until the proclamation of the French Empire, was always on the verge of revolt and its urban masses were a potential threat to any ruling government. The capital was also the main base of all the royalist and foreign spies who were active in France. The new Municipal Guard of Paris came into existence on 4 October 1802, consisting of two half-brigades (regiments after 1804) that were mostly recruited from older veterans of the French Army as well as former members of the Gendarmerie. These men were experienced soldiers or policemen, each of them having served for at least ten years and participated in at least five campaigns. The first half-brigade was tasked with guarding all the entrances to the French capital, while the second provided garrisons for various areas of the vast city. Attached to the two infantry units there was a squadron of dragoons, which patrolled the major streets and also acted as an honour guard when needed. Until 18 May 1806, the Municipal Guard of Paris was under the control of the city's civilian authorities, but from that date it was transferred to the authority of the Ministry of War. The two infantry demi-brigades each consisted of two battalions with five companies, while the squadron of dragoons

Trooper (left) and trumpeter (right) of the Paris Municipal Guard.

had just two mounted companies. From 1805, the first battalion of each half-brigade was sent to serve with the army and participated in campaigns until 1807 as part of the French Army's reserves. From 1808–12, the composite demi-brigade of the Municipal Guard serving with the army fought with great distinction in Spain, showing their valour as veteran soldiers. On 12 February 1812, the units that were stationed in Paris were reorganized as a single regiment of line infantry formed by two battalions, each of which latter had one company of grenadiers, one of voltigeurs (light infantrymen) and four of fusiliers. On 23 October 1812, while Napoleon was in Russia, the Municipal Guard of Paris participated in a failed military coup that was organized against the emperor by General Malet. This event marked the end of the corps, Napoleon reacting to the coup by returning to Paris and disbanding the Municipal Guard, its infantrymen being absorbed into the 134th Line Infantry Regiment. The squadron of dragoons, which had not taken part in the attempted coup, was absorbed into the Dutch Lancers of the Imperial Guard in February 1813. The dragoons of the Municipal Guard were uniformed like their equivalents of the army, but in light blue with red facings.

Chapter 10

Naval Units

History and organization

On 26 December 1774, after some failed experiments, the French Navy reorganized its troops on 100 companies of naval infantry (collectively known as the Corps Royal d'Infanterie de la Marine, or Royal Corps of Naval Infantry) and three companies of naval artillery (the Bombardiers de la Marine, or Naval Bombers). These units usually acted independently from each other and served on the various warships of the fleet. A single company of naval infantry comprised one lieutenant, two ensigns, one fourrier, six sergeants, six corporals, six lance-corporals, three drummers and ninety-six rankers, while each company of naval artillery had two lieutenants, two ensigns, one fourrier, two sergeants, four corporals, one drummer, twelve artificers and fifty bombardiers. In January 1786, the companies of naval infantry and naval artillery were combined to create a new Corps royal des cannoniers-matelots (Royal Corps of gunners-sailors), an attempt to consolidate the duties of naval infantrymen and artillerymen with those of the sailors. The cannoniers-matelots were trained in gunnery and the use of small arms, as well as in some aspects of the sailors' standard duties. The new corps was structured on nine divisions, one for each of the nine squadrons that made up the French Navy. Each division consisted of nine companies, and the ratio of cannoniers-matelots embarked on warships was to be seven for every ten guns (for example, a seventy-four-gun warship was to have about fifty-two such soldiers on board). On 14 June 1792, the new republican government disbanded the Corps royal des cannoniers-matelots, and in its place raised four regiments of naval infantry and two of naval artillery (thus ending the soldier-sailor experiment). The four regiments of naval infantry had two battalions each, a single battalion consisting of eight line companies plus one elite company of grenadiers. The two regiments of naval artillery each had two battalions, a single battalion comprising eight companies. In 1794, the French government decided to dissolve the naval infantry and naval artillery, but it soon became apparent that this was a major mistake, resulting in a decree forming a new Marine Artillery Corps on 25 October 1795. This was to consist of seven demi-brigades of three battalions, each battalion comprising nine companies. The new demi-brigades were garrisoned in the major bases of the French Navy: three at Brest, one at Lorient, one at Rochefort and two at Toulon. Under the new organization, no marine infantry units were to be part of the French Navy, since the naval artillerymen were to also act as naval infantry. On shore, for example, the naval artillery were to garrison ports and naval arsenals.

On 5 May 1803, Napoleon abolished the existing demi-brigades and consolidated them into four regiments, the first two of which had four battalions each, while the remaining two had just two battalions apiece. Each battalion consisted of six companies. The Marine Artillery Corps also comprised four companies of *ouvriers* or workers, which were augmented to six in 1805. By then, the four regiments of naval artillery were stationed at Brest, Rochefort, Lorient, Toulon and Genoa. After the disastrous Russian campaign, Napoleon had to rebuild his forces almost from scratch, and thus decided to employ his naval artillery regiments as regular line infantry units. On 24 January 1813, these were transferred from the Marine Department to the War Department and were reorganized as follows: the 1st Regiment on eight battalions, the 2nd Regiment on ten battalions, the 3rd Regiment on four battalions and the 4th Regiment on four battalions. A single battalion now consisted of six companies. Six of these battalions remained in the major ports, all the other units of naval artillery being assembled together to create a Marine Division that fought brilliantly as line infantry during the German campaign of 1813 and the French campaign of 1814. With the first restoration of the Bourbons, the marine artillery was reorganized on just three regiments and was given the new denomination of Corps royal des cannoniers de la Marine (Royal Corps of Naval Artillerymen). The *ouvriers* had a different history: in 1806 they were expanded to two regiments that were recruited from unemployed men, who were tasked with shipbuilding work as well as garrison duties. During the following years, another three such regiments were raised, but these units were all disbanded in June 1810. A new militarized corps of marine workers had been formed in 1808, initially consisting of just eighteen companies but later being expanded to eight battalions. Known as the Ouvriers militaires de la Marine (Naval Military Workers), they continued to exist until 1814 and took part in several military campaigns by providing field battalions.

Napoleon was never happy with his warships' crews, since they were – for the most part – undisciplined mobs. Consequently, in March 1808, he decided to militarize the sailors of the French Navy. They were assembled into fifty Bataillons de la Marine (Marine Battalions), each of which was assigned to a single ship of the line or to two frigates. All the battalions were numbered in progressive order and were divided into four companies of 120 sailors each plus staff. Each sailor was issued with a proper uniform, a musket and a bayonet. By 1811, the establishment of the Bataillons de la

NCO of the Ouvriers militaires de la Marine with M1812 uniform.

Marine had been increased to a total of eighty-five units; sixty-three of these were known as the Equipages de Haut-Bord (High Seas Crews) and served on the high seas, while the remaining twenty-two became the Equipages de Flotille (Flotilla Crews) and served along the coastline or on the major rivers of the empire. In March 1813, the Equipages de Flotille were abolished and absorbed into the Equipages de Haut-Bord. In January 1814, each battalion of sailors was required to send a company of sailors-gunners with 120 men to the army, due to the ongoing military emergency caused by the invasion of France. With the restoration of the Bourbons, the Equipages de Haut-Bord were temporarily disbanded, being briefly re-formed in 1815 as forty battalions with six companies each.

Uniforms and equipment

Members of the Corps royal des cannoniers-matelots were dressed quite similarly to the foot artillery, but with a peculiar headgear: a wide-brimmed black round hat with the front part of the brim turned up, and bearing a national cockade and pompom in the distinctive colour of each division. They also had a dark blue coat with red frontal lapels, round cuffs and turnbacks, collars in the distinctive colour of each division, a dark blue sleeveless waistcoat and trousers, plus black short gaiters laced up on the outside. The naval infantry regiments of 1792 were uniformed as follows: black bicorn with red pompom and national cockade, dark blue coat with frontal lapels, round cuffs and shoulder straps piped in red, a red collar, cuff flaps and turnbacks (the latter having white anchor badges), a dark blue waistcoat piped in red, dark blue trousers and black gaiters. The dress of the naval artillery regiments of 1792 included a Tarleton-type helmet with black crest and red plume, dark blue coat with frontal lapels piped in red, a red collar, round cuffs, epaulettes and turnbacks, dark blue waistcoat piped in red, dark blue trousers and black gaiters. The later demi-brigades wore a black bicorn with tricolour cockade, dark blue coat with red piping to front lapels, round cuffs and turnbacks, a red collar piped in white, red cuff flaps, a dark blue waistcoat, dark blue trousers and black gaiters. The Marine Artillery Corps of 1803 was given the following uniform: black bicorn with tricolour cockade, yellow cockade loop and red pompom, dark blue coat with red-piped frontal lapels, round cuffs and turnbacks, red collar piped in white, red cuff flaps and epaulettes, dark blue waistcoat, dark blue trousers and black gaiters. In 1807, the bicorn was replaced by a black shako with a red pompom, cords and flounders, the new headgear also having a brass plate on the front showing two crossed cannons under a flaming grenade. The *ouvriers* were dressed like the members of the Marine Artillery Corps, but with red frontal lapels. The Ouvriers militaires de la Marine formed in 1808 were uniformed like the naval artillerymen, but with black facings (collar, round cuffs and frontal lapels). The sailors of the Bataillons de la Marine wore a black shako with pompom in the distinctive colour of each battalion, white cords and flounders, and brass diamond-shaped frontal plate bearing unit number, along with a dark blue double-breasted jacket (*paletot*) with collar, round cuffs and shoulder straps in the distinctive colour of each battalion, a dark blue waistcoat, dark blue trousers (white during the summer months) and grey gaiters. The shako, which was hated by most of the sailors, was replaced in 1811 by a simpler black round hat.

Chapter 11

Colonial Units

When the French Revolution broke out in 1789, the nation had numerous colonies spread over three continents. These possessions were not vast in territory, but their economic importance was great so they were often envied by the other major European powers. Nearly all the French colonies owed their wealth to commerce and exploitation of local resources by slave labour, Haiti being the richest and most important of them due to its many plantations. French colonial possessions in 1789 included the following: Haiti, Martinique, Guadeloupe and some other smaller islands in the Caribbean region; Guyana on the northern coastline of South America; Isle-de-France (modern Mauritius) and Isle-de-Bourbon (Réunion)in the Indian Ocean; the city of Pondichéry in India; Senegal in Africa; and Saint-Pierre-et-Miquelon in the Atlantic Ocean. France had been a colonial power in North America until 1754, when the outbreak of the French–Indian War marked the beginning of the end for the French presence in the region. Before this conflict, France controlled a extensive portion of North America, corresponding to the eastern half of present-day Canada plus the vast and mostly unexplored region of Louisiana. Canada had been settled by the French since the early decades of the seventeenth century, while Louisiana had started to see the presence of some French hunters and merchants only shortly before the beginning of the French–Indian War. With their expansion across Louisiana directed towards the southern Gulf of Mexico, the French wanted to link their large Canadian possessions with the Caribbean, where they already had important colonies such as Haiti. They would thereby have controlled the course of the Mississippi and Missouri rivers, enabling them to connect Canada with the city of New Orleans, which, located on the delta of the Mississippi as well as on the Gulf of Mexico, would become an important commercial outpost thanks to its geographical position. These plans for the creation of a French empire in North America were frustrated by the course of the French–Indian War, which took place at the same time as the Seven Years' War in Europe. The conflict ended in disaster for the French: the British, who already controlled the areas surrounding the Bay of Hudson before 1754, conquered Canada and annexed it to their growing empire. The French also had to evacuate Louisiana, which was divided into two parts: the western portion (including New Orleans) was given to

Spain, while the eastern one was occupied by Great Britain. In consequence, France no longer had a colonial presence in North America by 1763, although it continued to have some flourishing island colonies in the Caribbean.

When the Thirteen Colonies rebelled against Britain in 1775, they had no regular army or navy to speak of, so they set out to form an alliance with France in order to gain the support of their military forces (which were then among the best and largest in Europe). The French monarchy, eager to take its revenge over the British in North America, immediately supported – diplomatically and financially – the Continental Congress legislative bodies of the colonists. Initially, however, the French refused to intervene militarily against Britain, since they were doubtful whether George Washington could lead the rebels to victory in the war. This changed after the Battle of Saratoga in 1777, which showed that the Continental Army was strong enough to face the British regulars on the open field and to defeat them. Thanks to the great efforts of the US ambassador in France, Benjamin Franklin, France signed a treaty of alliance with the colonists in March 1778 and thus entered the war. The French military contribution to the cause of the Thirteen Colonies was absolutely vital, the arrival of the French Navy in the North Atlantic allowing the Continental Congress to achieve its first important victories at sea. The French vessels transported large quantities of weapons and supplies to North America, which were essential for Washington's success. The French also despatched an expeditionary corps to the Thirteen Colonies, consisting of well-equipped and trained regulars, who took part in several major engagements and played a decisive role during the siege of Yorktown in 1781. The French also fought against the British in the Caribbean islands (also known at the time as the West Indies), as well as other areas of the world such as western Africa and India, where Britain and France had contrasting colonial interests. With the signing of the Treaty of Paris in 1783, which ended the American War of Independence, France regained the Caribbean island of Tobago and the African colony of Senegal from Britain. The western portion of Louisiana, meanwhile, was assigned to Spain, which had fought on France's side.

From the late seventeenth century, the colonial armed forces of France were under the control of the navy rather than the army. While each of the overseas territories listed above had an autonomous administration, its military forces were raised and supplied by the Ministry of the Navy in Paris. France's colonial troops were a separate entity from both the metropolitan army and the naval infantry/artillery, so army orders regarding structure of units, uniforms, pay, equipment and awards did not apply to them, their administration being controlled by the navy. Differently from the officers of the regular French Army, who were mostly aristocrats from the noble families of France, those of the colonial units could come from the lowest ranks of society and could earn their positions through their personal capabilities. Until 1760, the French Ministry of the Navy had administered a vast colonial empire on behalf of the king, but with the end of the Seven Years' War, most of the surviving colonial units had been absorbed into the regular army as the colonies in which they served had been occupied by the British. In 1762, it was decided that some regiments from the metropolitan army would serve as garrison units in the colonies that were still controlled by France. However, this measure was unpopular from the beginning because the ordinary French soldiers were not happy about the possibility of being deployed in far-flung and inhospitable outposts thousands of miles away from their homeland. French communities living in the various colonies were also against this decision, since the units garrisoning their settlements had always included a high percentage of men recruited locally and been commanded by officers who were colonists themselves. The aristocracy of France was not particularly loved in the colonies, which were inhabited by individuals who would have been at the margins of society in Europe.

As a result of the situation outlined above, the French government decided to reorganize the military garrisons of its colonies in 1766, forming several new units to be sent to the various overseas territories. The Regiment 'Du Cap' and Regiment 'Port-au-Prince' were established for service in Haiti (called Saint-Domingue by the French), while Martinique and Guadeloupe received one regiment each, as did Isle-de-France and Isle-de-Bourbon along with the city of Pondichéry. All these new units, seven in total, were to consist of two battalions and to comprise the soldiers already serving in their respective colonies plus some new recruits. In the end, however, only the new regiments in the Caribbean reached their planned establishments. In January 1775, the 'Isle-de-Bourbon' Regiment was abolished and its men were absorbed into the 'Isle-de-France' Regiment, which was expanded to four battalions. The 'Pondichéry' Regiment, which had been able to raise only a single battalion, was expanded with the recruiting of a battalion of local Indian soldiers (sepoys). After the decision to raise regiments in the various colonies was taken, Guyana and Senegal continued to be garrisoned by single battalions, as they had in recent years; it should be remembered that both these colonies only had small communities of French settlers and that a good portion of France's land in Senegal had been lost to the British during the Seven Years' War. The battalion garrisoning Guyana consisted of eight companies, which was increased to ten in 1779, while the battalion stationed in Senegal at Gorée was disbanded by 1775 and replaced by a half-company consisting of just fifty men (known as the Volontaires d'Afrique, or African Volunteers). Following the fall of Canada, France retained possession of just a small colony in North America: the island of Saint-Pierre-et-Miquelon in the

North Atlantic, south of Newfoundland. This was garrisoned by a small company of fifty soldiers. In addition to the infantry units described above, each of France's colonies usually had one or more artillery companies of Cannoniers-Bombardiers, tasked with manning the guns of the local fortifications.

The various colonial units did not have a standard internal organization, except for those serving in the West Indies and on Isle-de-France. These – the Regiment 'Du Cap', Regiment 'Port-au-Prince', Regiment 'Martinique', Regiment 'Guadeloupe' and Regiment 'Isle-de-France' – were structured on two battalions (except for the latter, which had four battalions). Each battalion consisted of one company of grenadiers, one company of chasseurs and eight companies of fusiliers. Grenadier and chasseur companies had the following internal establishment: one captain, one first lieutenant, one second lieutenant, one fourrier, two sergeants, four corporals, four lance-corporals, one drummer and forty rankers. Fusilier companies consisted of the following elements: one captain, one first lieutenant, one second lieutenant, one fourrier, four sergeants, eight corporals, eight lance-corporals, two drummers and fifty-six rankers. Each battalion had a staff comprising one battalion commander, one major, one assistant major, one sub-assistant major and two ensigns. There were eleven colonial artillery companies, each of them consisting of 105 officers and men, except for that stationed in Guyana (which numbered just fifty-three soldiers). Following the launch of the French Revolution, several of the colonial military units revolted against the new republican government, which decided to disband the colonial army inherited from the monarchy. From June 1792, it was decided that the colonial military forces would be reorganized as six regiments of line infantry, numbered 106–112, with the same structure and uniforms as the metropolitan infantry regiments. Listed below are the military units garrisoning each of the French colonies from 1792–1815, along with a brief outline of their history during the Napoleonic period.

Saint-Domingue (Haiti): In 1791, the black slaves of France's most important colony rose up in revolt against their colonial government, with the objective of obtaining the abolition of slavery. Supported by the Spaniards and the British, the rebels obtained a series of victories. The French were forced to concede freedom to all the black slaves of the island, but Haiti gradually became completely independent from France under the leadership of its great military commander, Toussaint Louverture, who gave nominal allegiance to the French Republic while pursuing his own political designs and governing as a military dictator. In 1801, Toussaint had himself named 'Governor-General' of Haiti, to which Napoleon responded by sending a large expeditionary force to the island. After several months of bitter fighting, however, the French were defeated by a combination of the black army of Touissant and the yellow fever. Haiti became an independent country on 1 January 1804.

Martinique: The original garrison consisted of the Regiment 'Martinique' (raised in 1772, with two battalions) plus three companies of Cannoniers-Bombardiers (formed in 1774 and serving also in Guadeloupe). The island was conquered by the British in March 1794. Following the Treaty of Amiens in 1802, Martinique was returned to France and started to be garrisoned by two regiments of metropolitan line infantry (the 26th and 82nd). The French troops were supplemented by the following auxiliary corps recruited locally: one company of black light infantry (Chasseurs volontaires de la Martinique), one company of gendarmerie, one company of artillery workers, one company of pioneers and six battalions of National Guard (each with one company of grenadiers, one company of chasseurs, eight companies of fusiliers and one company of dragoons).

Guadeloupe: The original garrison consisted of the Regiment 'Guadeloupe' (established in 1772, with two battalions) plus three companies of Cannoniers-Bombardiers (raised in 1774 and serving also in Martinique). The island was conquered by the British in 1810 and again in 1815, after it had been briefly returned to the French with the restoration of the Bourbons (its governor had sided with Napoleon following his return from exile on Elba). During the Napoleonic period, Guadeloupe was garrisoned by the 66th Line Infantry Regiment plus the following auxiliary corps recruited locally: three companies of black light infantry (Chasseurs de la Guadeloupe), a small detachment of gendarmerie, four companies of artillery workers and six battalions of National Guard (with one company of chasseurs, eight companies of fusiliers and one company of dragoons each).

Guyana: The original garrison consisted of the Battalion 'Cayenne' (raised in 1764 and consisting of four companies by 1789) plus one company of Cannoniers-Bombardiers (raised in 1764). In 1792, the Battalion 'Cayenne' was replaced by the 2nd Battalion of the 53rd Line Infantry Regiment. The latter was supplemented by a locally recruited Bataillon de la Guyane raised from local white settlers, as well as a company of black gendarmes and a company of black sappers. A joint Anglo-Portuguese expedition sailing from Brazil occupied French Guyana in 1809.

Louisiana: In 1803, Napoleon signed the Treaty of San Ildefonso with Spain, according to which the whole territory of Louisiana was given to France in exchange for some concessions that the First Consul made to the Spaniards in Italy. Before

Louisiana could receive its garrison of French soldiers, however, Napoleon decided to sell his newly acquired American colony to the United States of President Thomas Jefferson for $15 million. France was relieved of lands that it could neither develop nor properly defend, but earned a substantial sum of money that could be used to continue the wars in Europe. During the brief period of renewed French rule, the militia of Louisiana consisted of six companies of infantry recruited from white settlers, three companies of infantry recruited from blacks and mulattoes (mixed African and European parentage), two companies of cavalry and one company of artillery. These were supplemented by three companies of volunteer infantry, two of which were made up of French colonists and one of US colonists.

Saint-Pierre-et-Miquelon: The original garrison consisted of a single infantry company. The small Atlantic island was occupied by the British in May 1793.

Senegal: The original garrison of 1789 consisted of a single battalion with two companies, which was supplemented from 1799 by one Compagnie Auxiliare (Auxiliary Company) made up of black soldiers and by one company of local volunteers. The small French outposts in Senegal were all conquered by the British in July 1809.

Isle-de-France and Isle-de-Bourbon: The original garrison consisted of the Regiment 'Isle-de-France' (raised in 1772, with four battalions) and three companies of Cannoniers-Bombardiers (raised in 1764). The Regiment 'Isle-de-France' became the 107th Regiment of Line Infantry in 1792 before being completely reorganized in 1804, and was supported by the following auxiliary units: one battalion of volunteer light infantry recruited from Isle-de-Bourbon, one mounted squadron acting as the guard of the local governor, one small corps of gendarmerie, one detachment of artillery workers, one company of invalids, two battalions of sedentary militia recruited from Africans (tasked with guarding the plantations) and several units of National Guard (comprising white line infantrymen and black light infantrymen, in addition to some cavalry and artillery). In 1810, both Isle-de-France and Isle-de-Bourbon were invaded by the British.

India: The original garrison consisted of the Regiment 'Pondichéry' (comprising one white battalion raised in 1772 and one battalion of local sepoys formed in 1773) plus one company of Cannoniers-Bombardiers (established in 1776). The Indian city of Pondichéry was lost by the French in August 1793 when it was conquered by the British. In 1802, Napoleon re-raised the sepoy battalion and organized a military

Colonial Units 139

Private of the Sepoy Battalion in 1802, with the typical headgear and short trousers of the Indian native troops.

expedition to reconquer Pondichéry, but this ended in complete failure after having briefly restored the French presence in India.

Dutch colonies: At the outbreak of the Revolutionary Wars, the Dutch controlled a vast, commercially flourishing colonial empire. This comprised several islands in the Caribbean, Surinam in South America, Cape Colony in South Africa, Ceylon (modern Sri Lanka) and the rich 'Spice Islands' or Dutch East Indies that are known today as Indonesia. The Dutch state became a satellite of France in 1795, first as the Batavian Republic and later as the Kingdom of Holland. Consequently, between 1795 and 1810, most of the Dutch colonial territories were invaded by the British. By 1810, when Napoleon annexed the Kingdom of Holland to the French Empire, only Indonesia was still under Dutch control. The French tried to raise a large colonial force to defend the former Dutch East Indies that were now part of their colonial territories, but the British occupied Indonesia in 1811 before the French presence there could be a stabilized. During their brief period of rule, the French reorganized the military forces of the Dutch East Indies on the following lines: three regiments of line infantry with three battalions each, one regiment of light infantry with two battalions, one cavalry regiment, one regiment of foot artillery with three battalions, three regiments of garrison infantry with two battalions each and one independent battalion of garrison infantry.

Colonial units in France: On 16 August 1803, Napoleon ordered the raising of four Bataillons coloniaux (Colonial Battalions) in France, semi-penal units recruited from the worst elements of the French Army. The four battalions were used to garrison some isolated outposts of the French Empire and saw coastal defence action at various times during their history. The 1st Battalion was stationed on the island of Walcheren in the Netherlands, the 2nd Battalion in Corsica, the 3rd Battalion on Ile-de-Ré (off La Rochelle) and the 4th Battalion on Belle-Isle (to the south of Brittany). In 1811, a battalion of colonial pioneers was attached to each of the four Colonial Battalions, the new pioneer units being true punishment corps. In 1813, the Bataillons coloniaux were also transformed into pioneer units and were deprived of their weapons. From their foundation they had been dressed like line infantry, but in iron grey with red facings.

Chapter 12

Foreign Units

Since the days of Louis XIV, in the late seventeenth century, the French Army had always included a sizeable number of foreign units. During the Revolutionary Wars, many foreign volunteers went to France in order to fight under the flag of the new Republic and soon became an important component of the French forces. Napoleon, after becoming First Consul in 1799, continued the French policy of having substantial numbers of foreigners in the military and sponsored the formation of several new corps made up of non-French soldiers. What follows is a brief outline of the French Army's foreign units that comprised some elements of cavalry or artillery/technical corps:

Neuchatel Battalion: In 1806, the small Principality of Neuchatel, located in northwest Switzerland, was ceded to France by Prussia. Napoleon, instead of annexing the small state to France, decided to give it as a reward to his Chief-of-Staff, Marshal Berthier (who became Prince of Neuchatel). On 11 May 1807, the armed forces of the Principality of Neuchatel were organized as a single line infantry battalion with six companies: one of grenadiers, one of voltigeurs (light infantry) and four of fusiliers (each with 160 men). Attached to the battalion was a mixed company of artillery and engineers consisting of the following elements: four officers, fourteen NCOs, thirty-two gunners, sixteen train drivers and sixteen sappers. The company was equipped with two 6-pounder guns. The Neuchatel Battalion served with distinction on several occasions, especially in Spain, until being officially disbanded in June 1814.

Italian Legion: In the spring of 1799, the Cisalpine Republic, the puppet state of France that had been created by Napoleon in northern Italy in 1797, was temporarily invaded by Austro-Russian forces. The large Cisalpine Army was disbanded following the fall of the republic, but many of its members followed the French during their retreat since they wanted to continue serving under Napoleon. As a result, the First Consul decided to create an Italian Legion within the French Army, made up of former Cisalpine soldiers. The new unit, formed on 8 September 1799, comprised four battalions of line infantry and four squadrons of mounted chasseurs, as well as one company of light artillery. Each of the infantry battalions had one

Gunner of the Neuchatel Battalion's artillery.

company of grenadiers, one company of chasseurs and eight companies of fusiliers. In January 1800, another two battalions were added to the existing ones, but the Italian Legion was disbanded after a few weeks when the Cisalpine Republic was restored by Napoleon following his victory at the Battle of Marengo.

Piedmontese Legion: In 1799, what remained of the Piedmontese Army was absorbed into the French Army when Piedmont (officially known as the Kingdom of Sardinia) was annexed to France. The Piedmontese soldiers were reorganized on two demi-brigades of line infantry, one demi-brigade of light infantry, one regiment of dragoons and one regiment of mounted chasseurs. However, these units were soon disbanded and none of them was still in existence by 1803. The pre-1799 Piedmontese Army also included five line infantry regiments of experienced Swiss mercenaries, whom the French tried to retain in service by reorganizing them on two legions, but these too were very short-lived. On 18 May 1803, Napoleon ordered the formation of four legions made up of former Piedmontese soldiers who were to be recruited from the Italian departments of the French Republic. Each legion was to comprise three battalions of line infantry, two battalions of light infantry and one company of artillery. Each battalion would have consisted of one elite company of grenadiers/carabiniers and four companies of fusiliers/chasseurs. Ultimately, however, only one of the four planned legions could be formed, this becoming known as the Piedmontese Legion or Légion du Midi. This formation served in Haiti before being reduced, in 1808, to just a single battalion of light infantry (with one company of carabiniers, one of voltigeurs and three of chasseurs).

Hanoverian Legion: Following the French occupation of Hanover, a German state governed by the same royal family that ruled Great Britain, Napoleon decided in 1803 to organize a legion made up of former members of the recently disbanded Hanoverian Army who wanted to serve under his flag. This new Hanoverian Legion was intended to have consisted of one light infantry regiment (with two battalions) and one regiment of mounted chasseurs (with four squadrons), but desertion and sickness prevented the corps from reaching its planned establishment. The unit did however serve in Spain during the following years, where it performed auxiliary functions. On 10 March 1810, the Westphalian Battalion (another foreign unit) was absorbed into the Hanoverian Legion, which could then finally reach the planned establishment of two battalions. The corps was finally disbanded on 11 August 1811, having suffered severe losses in Spain.

Portuguese Legion: The French Army occupied Portugal in 1807 after the country refused to close its ports to the Royal Navy and British merchant ships. Once the

Trooper of the Hanoverian Legion's cavalry.

Trooper of the Hanoverian Legion's cavalry.

Uniforms of the Portuguese Legion's infantry (left) and cavalry (right).

Portuguese Army was disbanded, Napoleon decided to reorganize it as a 9,000-strong Portuguese Legion to be part of the French Army. The new corps was established on 12 November 1807 and initially comprised five regiments of line infantry, one battalion of light infantry, three regiments of mounted chasseurs, one battery of artillery, one depot battalion of infantry and one depot squadron of cavalry. Many Portuguese soldiers swiftly deserted during their journey from Spain to France, and thus the Portuguese Legion was reduced to just three regiments of line infantry, one regiment of mounted chasseurs and one depot battalion of infantry. The corps served with distinction in the Austrian campaign of 1809 and took part in the Russian campaign of 1812. The Portuguese soldiers fought with great determination in Russia and were much admired by Napoleon. In 1813, after returning to France, the Portuguese Legion was further reduced to only two battalions of infantry (one active and one depot), and these were disbanded on 5 May 1814 following the first abdication of Napoleon.

Polish Legions: The Poles were among the most numerous and loyal foreign soldiers of Napoleon's army. They fought under the flag of the French Republic and later of the French Empire because they had one great objective: freeing their homeland from the foreign troops that had occupied it. In 1795, the Commonwealth of Poland and Lithuania had disappeared from the maps of Europe when it was partitioned between three great powers: Austria, Prussia and Russia. These nations were all hated by the Polish population and were also at war with Revolutionary France; as a result, Poland and France had several enemies in common. After a last Polish national uprising was crushed in 1794, thousands of Polish patriots who had fought for their freedom left their homeland as political refugees and travelled to France. Here they were organized into a Polish Legion that was intended to fight alongside the French, but since the new constitution of the French Republic did not allow the presence of foreign units in the French Army, the Polish Legion was transferred to the recently established Cisalpine Army of northern Italy. The Polish soldiers fought extremely well on several occasions and were admired by Napoleon, and thanks to their successes and the arrival of hundreds more volunteers, a 2nd Polish Legion was set up as part of the Cisalpine Army. The Poles suffered great losses in Italy in 1799 when the Allies organized an effective counter-offensive while Napoleon was in Egypt. The 2nd Polish Legion was completely destroyed and ceased to exist, while the 1st Legion was greatly reduced in its numbers.

With the temporary fall of the Cisalpine Republic, Napoleon decreed, after his return to France, that foreign troops could now serve as part of the French Army. The survivors of the 1st Polish Legion were thus reorganized as part of the Italian

Legion and a new Danube Legion was formed on the Rhine by recruiting new Polish volunteers (mostly PoWs from the Austrian Army). The Danube Legion was the first Polish military unit of the French Army, consisting of four line infantry battalions, four squadrons of lancers and one company of mounted artillery. The corps served on the Rhine and later fought at the Battle of Marengo. In December 1801, the 1st Polish Legion and the Danube Legion were brought together and reorganized as three demi-brigades of infantry: the 1st Polish, 2nd Polish and 3rd Polish half-brigades. The first two of these were made up of former members of the 1st Polish Legion, while the third comprised those who had been with the Danube Legion. The 2nd Polish and 3rd Polish demi-brigades were sent to Haiti by Napoleon in 1802, where they were completely destroyed by the island's rebels and by yellow fever.

In 1805, the 1st Polish half-brigade was renamed the 1st Polish Legion and assigned to the army of the Kingdom of Italy (the direct heir of the Cisalpine Republic). In 1806, the Polish Legion, now consisting of just one line infantry regiment and one lancer regiment, was transferred to the army of the Kingdom of Naples (recently conquered by the French). After a few months in southern Italy, however, the corps was disbanded. During the 1807 war against Russia, Napoleon decided to raise a new Polish Legion from the many Polish PoWs who had previously served in the Prussian Army. This unit was known as the Northern Legion and was planned to consist of two sub-legions with four infantry battalions each; in the end, however, only one sub-legion came into existence. The latter served with distinction until 1808, when it was absorbed into the army of the newly constituted Grand Duchy of Warsaw. After great sacrifices, during 1807/08 the Poles fighting for Napoleon had finally achieved their main objective: the creation of a new and independent Polish state in their homeland. Before the birth of the Grand Duchy of Warsaw, which was a protectorate of the French Empire, Napoleon decided to raise a new and larger Polish legion as part of the French Army. He assembled the former members of the Polish Legion who were no longer in Neapolitan service with new volunteers and – in February 1807 – was able to organize a new Legion of the Vistula that comprised three regiments of line infantry and one regiment of lancers. After having been part of the army of the Kingdom of Westphalia for a short period, the Vistula Legion was finally included among the units of the French Army on 21 February 1808. Two of its infantry regiments participated in the invasion of Spain, together with the lancer regiment, the latter being disbanded in 1811 and transformed into a newly organized French cavalry regiment (see Chapter 4). The years spent in Spain saw the Polish soldiers distinguishing themselves on several occasions.

Foreign Units

Trooper of the 1st Lancer Regiment of the Vistula Legion (later the 7th Regiment of Lancers).

In 1809, after having defeated the Austrians at the Battle of Wagram, Napoleon decreed the formation of a 2nd Vistula Legion recruited from Polish PoWs who had previously been part of the Austrian Army. This new unit consisted of just two infantry battalions and one lancer regiment and was very short-lived, being disbanded in February 1810. Its infantrymen became the 4th Infantry Regiment of the 1st Vistula Legion, while its cavalrymen were transformed into a French lancer regiment

Trooper of the Croatian Hussars.

(see Chapter 4). In 1812, in preparation for the invasion of Russia, the number of battalions in each infantry regiment of the Vistula Legion was increased from two to three, while a small battery with two 3-pounder guns was attached to each infantry regiment. Of the 7,000 Polish soldiers who followed Napoleon into Russia, only 1,500 returned. In consequence, the Vistula Legion was reorganized as the single Vistula Regiment (having two battalions) on 18 June 1813. With the restoration of the Bourbons in 1814, the Vistula Regiment was disbanded.

Croatian Hussars: During the Napoleonic period, the French occupied – albeit for short periods – several areas of the Balkans and recruited a number of military units there. The French controlled the following territories in the Balkans during the period 1797–1815: the Ionian Islands (also known as the Seven Islands, for a first period from 1797–99 and then from 1807–14), Dalmatia and Istria (which were annexed to the Kingdom of Italy for the period 1805–09 and then to the French Empire from 1809–14) and the Illyrian Provinces (which were part of the French Empire between 1809 and 1814). On 23 February 1813, a regiment of hussars was raised by the French from the border regions of Croatia, consisting of six squadrons with two troops each and being equipped at the expense of the citizens of the Illyrian Provinces. The unit took part in some minor military actions before being disbanded in November 1813. The surviving elements of the regiment were reorganized as five companies of Croatian Pioneers, which were dissolved in April 1814.

Black Pioneers: On 11 May 1803, Napoleon decided to create a Pionniers Noirs Battalion (Battalion of Black Pioneers) for the French Army by assembling together several coloured PoWs from the Caribbean island of Haiti (former supporters of the revolutionary leader Touissant Louverture) and a short-lived battalion of African Chasseurs that had been formed for the Indian campaign of 1803. The battalion served with distinction in Italy, and in August 1806 was transferred to the Neapolitan Army of which it became part (the Kingdom of Naples was at the time a puppet state of France, ruled by Napoleon's brother Joseph). In November 1806, the corps was transformed into a regiment of line infantry known as the Real Africano (Royal African).

Private of the Pionniers Noirs Battalion.

Bibliography

Brnardic, V., *Napoleon's Balkan Troops* (Osprey Publishing, 2004).
Bucquoy, E.L., *Dragons et Guides d'Etat-Major* (Editions Grancher, 1977–85).
Bucquoy, E.L., *Fanfares et Musiques* (Grancher, 1977–85).
Bucquoy E.L., *Gardes d'honneur et troupes étrangères* (Grancher, 1977–85).
Bucquoy, E.L., *La Cavalerie légère* (Grancher, 1977–85).
Bucquoy, E.L., *Le Passepoil* (Grancher, 1977–85).
Bucquoy, E.L., *Les Cuirassiers* (Grancher, 1977–85).
Bukhari E., *Napoleon's Cuirassiers and Carabiniers* (Osprey Publishing, 1977).
Bukhari E., *Napoleon's Dragoons and Lancers* (Osprey Publishing, 1976).
Bukhari E., *Napoleon's Hussars* (Osprey Publishing, 1978).
Bukhari E., *Napoleon's Line Chasseurs* (Osprey Publishing, 1977).
Chartrand, R., *Napoleon's Overseas Army* (Osprey Publishing, 1989).
Chartrand, R., *Napoleon's Sea Soldiers* (Osprey Publishing, 1990).
Dempsey, G.C., *Napoleon's mercenaries: Foreign Units in the French Army under the Consulate and Empire 1799 to 1814* (Frontline Books, 2016).
Elting, J.R., *Napoleonic Uniforms* (Pearson, 1993–2000).
Elting, J.R., *Swords around a Throne: Napoleon's Grande Armée* (Free Press, 1988).
Fieffé, E., *Histoire des Troupes Etrangères au Service de France* (Librairie Militaire, 1854).
Funcken, F. and Funcken, L., *Les Soldats de la Revolution Française* (Casterman, 1988).
Greentree, D. and Campbell, D., *Napoleon's Swiss Troops* (Osprey Publishing, 2012).
Haythornthwaite, P., *Napoleon's Specialist Troops* (Osprey Publishing, 1988).
Haythornthwaite, P., *Uniforms of the Peninsular War 1807–1814* (Blandford Press, 1978).
Haythornthwaite, P., *Uniforms of the Retreat from Moscow 1812* (Blandford Press, 1976).
Haythornthwaite, P., *Uniforms of Waterloo* (Blandford Press, 1986).
Morawski, R. and Dusiewicz, A., *The Polish Army under Napoleon's command* (Karabela Publishing, 2010).
Pawly, R., *Napoleon's Carabiniers* (Osprey Publishing, 2005).
Wilkinson-Latham, R., *Napoleon's Artillery* (Osprey Publishing, 1975).

Index

Black Pioneers, 151

Croatian Hussars, 151

Danube Legion, 148

Guadeloupe, 137
Guyana, 137

Hanoverian Legion, 143

Italian Legion, 141, 143

Louis XIV, 14, 15, 28, 57, 141
Louisiana, 137, 138

Martinique, 137

Neuchatel Battalion, 141
Ney, 7

Paris Guard, 125, 126, 127
Piedmontese Legion, 143
Polish Legion, 147
Portuguese Legion, 143, 147

Saint-Domingue, 136
Senegal, 138

Vistula Legion, 148, 149, 151